Elements of Second and Foreign Languages Teaching to Indigenous Learners of Canada

Peter Lang

Bruxelles · Bern · Berlin · New York · Oxford · Wien

Pierre Demers

Elements of Second and Foreign Languages Teaching to Indigenous Learners of Canada

Theories, Strategies and Practices

Champs didactiques plurilingues
Vol. 5

Special thanks to Mrs. Josée Simard from the Université du Québec à Chicoutimi, Mrs. Cynthia Björk from the Santa Fe Public Schools, Dr. Gabriela Grigoroiu from the Cree School Board and Dr. Gregory Nutefe Kwadzo formerly from the Kahnawà:ke Education Center for their help in reviewing former versions of the book.

This publication has been peer reviewed.

Any representation or reproduction, in whole or in part, made by any means whatsoever, without the consent of the publisher or his successors in title, is illegal. All rights reserved.

© P.I.E. PETER LANG s.a.
 Éditions scientifiques internationales
 Bruxelles, 2021
 1 avenue Maurice, B-1050 Bruxelles, Belgique
 www.peterlang.com ; brussels@peterlang.com

ISSN 2593-6972
ISBN 978-2-8076-1872-5
ePDF 978-2-8076-1873-2
ePub 978-2-8076-1874-9
DOI 10.3726/b18409
D/2021/5678/35

Bibliographic Information published by the Deutsche Nationalbibliothek

The Deutsche Nationalbibliothek lists this publication in the Deutsche Nationalbibliografie; detailed bibliographic data is available online at http://dnb.d-nb.de.

Dedication

To my all my family members who came from Africa, America, Asia and Europe and found ways to communicate and interact with their different languages and cultures

Table of Contents

Figures 13

Tables 15

Acknowledgments 17

Introduction 19

Part I: Theoretical Considerations

Chapter 1: Definitions of Concepts of L2 Didactics 25
    The Concept of Language 25
    The Concepts of L1 and L2 29
    Example: Cree in Québec 30
    Canada's Official and Aboriginal Languages 32
    The Concept of Culture 33
    The Concept of L2 Learner 35
    The Concept of L2 Teacher 35
    The Concepts of L2 Teaching and Learning 36
    The Concept of L2 Method 37
    The Concept of L2 Didactics Paradigms 37

Chapter 2: Eurocentric L2 Didactics Paradigms 39
    Historical Aspect 39
    Pedagogical Aspect 42
    The Action-Oriented Approach 44
    The Neurolinguistics Approach 44
    The Radical Approach 45

Chapter 3: Descriptions of Eurocentric L2 Didactics Paradigms 47

    The Classical Paradigm 47
    Typical Teaching Procedures for a Classical Lesson 48
    The Progressivist Paradigm 49
    Typical Teaching Procedures for a Progressivist Lesson .. 50
    The Behaviorist Paradigm 50
    Typical Teaching Procedures for a Behaviorist Lesson 51
    The Communicative Paradigm 52
    Typical Teaching Procedures for a Communicative
        Lesson 54
    The Immersion Programs 55
    The Radical Paradigm 56
    Typical Teaching Procedures for a Radical Lesson 62
    Beyond the Concepts of L2 Didactics Paradigms 63
    Questions to Explore the L2 Didactics Paradigms 65

Chapter 4: A Suggested L2 Didactics Paradigm for Aboriginal Learners 67

    Elements of Aboriginal Teaching 67
    The Wheels 73
    The Circles 75
    Suggestions for L2 Teaching to Aboriginal Peoples 76
    A Successful Experience of L2 Teaching
        to Cree Learners 76
    Exclusive Use of Oral Language 77
    A Trustful Relationship 77
    The Four Facets of a Person 78
    Teacher's Awareness of Learners' Needs 78
    A Strong Self-Esteem 79
    The Use of Many Senses 79
    Learning Is a Group Process 79
    Integration of Aboriginal Cultures in the Class 79

Table of Contents

Part II: Practical Considerations

Chapter 5: Before Teaching Procedures 85
    Class Preparation 85
    The L2 Program 85
    The Technology 86
    Learning Objects 87
    Classroom Layout 88
    Preparation to Class 88
    Transactional Distance 88

Chapter 6: Teaching Procedures 91
    Teaching the Oral Component of the Language 91
    Teaching Listening Skills 91
    Teaching Speaking Skills 93
    Teaching Interaction Skills 94
    An Induced Daydream: The Forest 95
    Teaching the Written Component of the Language 96
    Teaching Reading Skills 97
    Teaching Writing Skills 99
    An Induced Daydream: The Beach 100
    Lesson Zero 101
    Suggested L2 Teaching Procedures 102
    Procedures for Illiterate Beginners 103
    Procedures for Beginners 105
    Procedures for Intermediate Learners 108
    Procedures for Advanced Learners 110

Chapter 7: After Teaching Procedures 113
    Correction of Errors 113
    Oral Errors Correction with the Help of Gestures 115
    Writing Errors Correction 116
    Phonetic Correction 117

        Basics of Verbotonal Phonetics 117
        Testing 119

Conclusion 123

References 125

Annex I: **L2 Teaching to Aboriginal Learners in Québec** 135
        Historical Perspective 135
        Geographical Perspective 136

Annex II: **Teaching French L2 to Different L1 Learners** 139

Annex III: **IPA Transcription of the Québec Cree** 141
        Québec Cree Phonemes 142

Afterword 143

Book Summary 145

About the Author 147

Figures

Fig. 1: Constituent Concepts of L2 Didactics Paradigms 38
Fig. 2: Spread of the Classical Paradigm 40
Fig. 3: A Traditional Aboriginal Education Wheel 74

Tables

Tab. 1: Approximate Dates of the Rising of the Eurocentric Paradigms in L2 Didactics History 42

Tab. 2: Aims of Eurocentric L2 Didactics Paradigms 65

Tab. 3: Relations between Learners' Linguistic Levels and Elements of Procedures 111

Acknowledgments

I wish to thank all the students I taught either French or English all over Canada and abroad and, in a particular way, Mrs. Christine Coonishish Mattawashish, Mrs. Laurie Ann Mianscum Brien and Mr. John Wapachee, my Bush People[1] of Mistissini[2] for their desire to learn that inspired me to write this book.

I also wish to thank future L2 teachers and teachers I taught all over Canada or abroad and who asked me questions that inspired me. A special thank you goes to my linguistics students from the *Université de Moncton, campus d'Edmundston (UMCE)* and my education students from the *Université Sainte Anne*.

---

[1] A person who was born and raised in the bush, away from Eurocentric culture.
[2] The easternmost Cree community of Québec and therefore of North America.

Introduction

Being able to speak a second or a foreign language has always been a necessity for many people and the intense globalization period we are living in will even increase that necessity.

In the Antiquity already, languages such as Latin, Greek, Aramaic, Sanskrit or Mandarin were communication tools for peoples from different mother tongues depending on their needs and the areas they came from.

This book is intended for practicing or future language teachers and, more generally, for everyone who is interested in second or foreign (L2[3]) language teaching to Aboriginal[4] learners (however not exclusively).

The book is an essay. That is the reason why the style differs from a traditional scholar book or even a textbook. Also, the book is written in a more personal style as it is a testimony of the author's expertise and experience as a researcher and teacher in the area of L2 teaching to students of various academic levels, from children to adults and, of course, to Aboriginal learners. Indeed, if there are books on the market that deal with L2 didactics and methodologies in general, (Howatt with Widdowson, 2004; Puren, 1988; Varga, 2014; Cuq and Gruca, 2018, for example) no book specifically targets the L2 Aboriginal learner.

If the L2 paradigms described in the book do exist in L2 didactics nowadays, the way to understand them is subjective and could be seen in a different manner by other didacticians. The L2 teaching techniques suggested and described in the book are not all the techniques that could be used by a L2 teacher. All the testimonies presented come from the personal experience of the author.

---

[3] L2 symbol is used when we refer to a foreign or a second language while the symbol L1 is used when we refer to a dominant language or a mother tongue.

[4] In Canada, Indigenous Peoples are generally called Aboriginal Peoples by the Federal government, the words Indigenous Peoples referring to Native Peoples from other countries. Those terms will be further explained later in the text.

As a matter of fact, the book was written wishing that, reading it, current or future language teachers would have a better idea of different theories and practices that are found today in the field and will therefore be able to improve their teaching and, hopefully, their learners' and more specifically their Aboriginal learners' performances.

Moreover, L2 teaching is an artistic as well a scientific discipline. Indeed, if there are underlying theories to diverse L2 approaches, the domain requires from the L2 teacher a good deal of attitudes, skills and reflexes most often inspired by the teacher's judgment, personality, expertise and experience.

The book is therefore mainly a series of thoughts, considerations and testimonies inspired by the author's professional life as a researcher in L2 didactics and as a French and English L2 teacher, because it is firmly believed that the description of real events can touch the readers who will then be able to relate those events to their own professional life.

The book is divided in two parts, the theoretical considerations and the practical considerations, since it is of great importance for L2 teachers to have a general understanding of the theories underlying the methods they use in order for them to know why they do what they do in the classroom.

In the first part, the theoretical considerations, key concepts will be defined because some of them, although seemingly very clear, may vary according to different L2 methods and paradigms.

Then, an overview of important Eurocentric trends or paradigms that emerged for different reasons at various times in L2 didactics history will also be given and Eurocentric L2 didactics paradigms will be described as it seems possible to group most of L2 methods in use today according to their aims, therefore helping the language teacher to be able to understand them more clearly and to use them in a proper context. The Eurocentric paradigms described in the book are the classical paradigm (often called the grammar-translation method), the progressivist paradigm, the behaviorist paradigm, the communicative paradigm (including the action-oriented and the neurolinguistic approaches) and the radical paradigm. As the radical paradigm has been less described by authors than other paradigms, its description will be more thorough than the description of the other paradigms. The radical paradigm is also the best suited for Aboriginal learners[5] because it addresses the whole person, as explained later in the book.

---

[5] For example, see Rahan (2009) on best practices with Aboriginal learners.

Introduction

To complete the first part, a literature review of traditional Aboriginal teaching will be made and L2 strategies to improve L2 teaching to Aboriginal learners will be given. That portion is the most important one for L2 teachers with no experience in the teaching of an L2 to Aboriginal learners.

In the second part, the practical considerations, a variety of procedures that can be used by L2 teachers before, during and after their teaching will be described. The procedures that can be used before teaching described is this book are the class preparation and the preparation to class.

The procedures that can be used in teaching described in this book are the teaching of listening skills, of speaking skills, of interaction skills, of reading skills and of writing skills.

The procedures that can be used after teaching described in this book are the correction of oral errors with gestures, the teaching of pronunciation with the verbotonal method, the correction of writing mistakes and the use of different types of language testing.

Part I:

Theoretical Considerations

In this part, a theoretical frame will be proposed in order for L2 teachers to have an overview of the diversity of the theoretical bases of different L2 teaching conceptions in use today and to understand the reasons why they teach what they teach. This part will also provide ways to improve L2 teaching to Aboriginal learners.

Chapter 1

Definitions of Concepts of L2 Didactics

The Concept of Language

In order to understand the concepts of L1 and L2, it is important to know what a language is.

A language is a set of arbitrary relations between mental images and sounds for the oral language and written signs for the written language.[6] Meaningful or functional sounds of a language are called the phonemes of the language, while its set of words is called its lexicon and its set of rules is called its syntax or grammar. The words of a language may be grouped in bigger units called clauses, sentences, paragraphs and texts providing specific rules are followed.

A language is the preferred communication tool for human beings and almost all of them speak at least one, their mother tongue, the one they learned when they were infants and, most often, from their mother. The communication in a language can be broken by many factors, the most important one being noise.

A language is also one of the most important developmental agents for infants because it gives access to the culture related to that language of which it is also one of the major manifestations. Indeed, a language influences the perceptions of the person who speaks it to such an extent that it is often difficult to imagine that an idea can be expressed in a way that differs from the one a person is used to.

Moreover, a language is also one of the most important socialization tools a person can use: it allows individuals to find their place among others, in their family and gradually thereafter in the society in general. It is

---

[6] See Saussure (1965) for a discussion of that topic.

by using a language that infants and children will learn who their mother is, who their parents and family members are, to know those they have to obey, those they have to fear, those they have to respect and those they can get closer to and who will become friends, even close friends. It is also through a language that infants and children will find their identity, their feelings of belonging to a group, a nation and a country.

Languages spoken in the world are very numerous and often differ a great deal from one another and it is not possible, with all the knowledge we have now, to know whether, at the dawn of humankind, only one language was spoken or whether it was more than one.[7]

It is customary, since the discovery of Sanskrit by Europeans in the eighteen century of our era, to classify languages in groups and families: French, Spanish, Portuguese and Italian belong to the Roman or Latin group for example, while English and German belong to the German group, Russian and Ukrainian belong to the Slavic group, those three groups belonging to the same family, the Indo-European family from which they are derived with other languages such as Hindi and Punjabi.

There are many other language families such as the Algic family, of which the Algonquin group, comprising, among others, Cheyenne, Ojibwa and Cree, is a member.

Languages of a same group or family share certain phonological, lexical and syntactic traits. That way, it is possible to regroup most languages, although a few languages such as Basque (a minority language spoken in France and Spain) remain isolated for unknown reasons.

If we take into account not only a language itself but also the way it is used in the culture it belongs to and that shapes it, as tenants of the New Communication do,[8] as we will see below, languages can be classified according to extra or paralinguistic criteria that, when respected, contribute to verbal communication. For instance criteria are: the presence or absence of gestures and of touching one another when speaking, the optimal distance in which people feel at ease when speaking and, in a broad way, the notion of time shared by people speaking the same language.

---

[7] See Ruhlen (1994) for a discussion of that topic.
[8] See Hall (1959, 1966) and Birdwhistell (1960) for further discussion of the topic.

Combining those criteria, it is possible to distinguish languages of type *A*, the warm climate languages, from languages of type *B*, the cold climate languages as Lanier (2000) does.

In type *A* languages, people make more gestures, touch more one another and are closer to each other when they speak than in type *B* languages; in type *A* languages, the speakers have a more cyclical perception of time than in type *B* languages where the speakers have a more linear perception of time. Speakers from type *A* languages tend to do many things at the same time and also tend not to respect a schedule imposed by outside elements, such as a watch, while speakers from type *B* languages tend to do one thing at a time and to respect a schedule coming from outside.

In that way, French, Spanish and Arabic belong to type *A* languages while English, German and Japanese belong to type *B* languages. Many languages, though, have traits of both types: for example, Québec Cree is a mixed type language, because the perception its speakers have of time is highly cyclical, even though they do not touch one another and make very few gestures when they speak to each other.

It is also important to note that the mastery of the linguistic code alone does not suffice to ensure good communication between people. Using the criteria just mentioned contributes on a more or less conscious level to the delivery of the verbal communication message with comfort.

For example, in most languages, there are many ways of speaking depending on whom we are talking to and in what context. We choose different registers when we speak to friends or strangers: in French, for example, we more easily use the word '*tu*' (you) in the first instance and the word '*vous*' (you) in the last instance while in English, we use more contractions in the first instance than in the last instance. We also use different levels of language whether we are in a bar or a classroom: no matter the language, individuals more willingly use a more familiar language in a bar than in a classroom where they more willingly use a more formal language, a form of the language that is closer to the written language.

Of course, all the different levels of a language have their own specificities. In English, for instance, the familiar language is full of regionalisms and contractions that are not so present in the normal language and even less in the formal language.

Major international languages such as Arabic, English, French, Mandarin, Spanish or Russian, which are spoken in different countries, also have different varieties: people do not speak English the same way in New York as they do in London, Toronto or Sydney no more than they speak French in Montreal the same way they do in Paris or Brussels, but they nevertheless speak the same language. As a matter of fact, it is impossible to sustain that a specific variety is superior to another one, that London English is superior to or better than Toronto or Newfoundland English, or that Paris French is superior to or better than Montreal or Geneva French.

As for French, there is a myth, at least in English Canada, that Paris French is superior to other varieties of French. That myth has to be destroyed because it renders the work of Québec or Canadian or even non Parisian French language teachers more difficult.[9]

The following testimony is an illustration of that problem.

Testimony 1: An English Canadian Convinced that Quebec French Is not Good French

The following event happened in the Vancouver area:
"I am in my office in a Canadian university where I teach French as a L2 when a student knocks at my door. I let him through and offer him to have a seat.
'I came to see you because I want to take a course to get rid of my little Quebec accent.'

– *'...'*
– *'I went to Quebec last summer for a French course and I learned Quebec accent'*
– *'Quebec accent is not a disease, you know.'*
– *'...'*
– *Anyhow, you are not talking to the right person because I am from Quebec. I would not try to lose my accent because it would mean losing my roots'*
– *'...'*
– *'What would you say if I were to tell you that I wish to lose my Canadian accent?'*
– *'That is not the same thing.'*
– *'Why'*

---

[9] In that way, French differs from other international languages such as English, Spanish or Portuguese in which, the myth of a superior variety is not strong: of course, L2 students may prefer a specific variety over another.

- *'Canadian English is English while Quebec French is not French.'*
- *'What makes you say that?'*
- *'Well, everybody knows that.'*
- *'Well, I don't know that and I am telling you it is not the case.'*

'Pierre Trudeau himself, the former Prime Minister of Canada, recognized that for a fact when he said that, in Quebec, they speak a lousy French and he was from Quebec.'

- *'I know, and it played a big part in that problem. But what do you want to do about your French class?'*
- *'I would like to take one of your courses because you speak good French.'*
- *'...'*

The student stands up and goes leaves convinced he knows what good French is. I hope never to see him again. I have to recognize that Pierre Trudeau is not the only one who encouraged that myth because some of my colleagues believe the same thing and, in their case, it is even worse because they are French."

The Concepts of L1 and L2

The first and often the only language someone learns is his or her mother tongue or L1, while all the other languages learned are his or her second or foreign languages or L2. Indeed, the L2 concept encompasses a third language (L3), a fourth language (L4) and so on. In fact, the concepts of L1 and L2 refer to ' ... two sets of terms-like such words as "left" and "right" ' (Stern, 1984, p. 9). In fact, L1 and L2 constitute a dichotomy in Stern's conception, a dichotomy that is widely used today in the field of language didactics.

Whatever the L2, its learning will always be influenced by the L1, the proximity of both languages, the knowledge the learner has of his or her L1 and so on.

However, if in many social contexts, the difference between those two concepts of L1 and L2 seems clear, it is not always the case. When the mother tongue of the individual is spoken by the vast majority of his or her fellow citizens (for instance English in the United States, French in France or Mandarin in China), it is easier for him or her to relate to that mother tongue. However, when his or her mother tongue is not spoken by the majority of the population (for instance French in English Canada or Cree in Québec and English Canada), the individual often has identity problems.

It is important here to remember that a few languages dominate the whole world. As a matter of fact, Arabic, English, French, Mandarin, Russian and Spanish,[10] for example, are widely spoken by people who also speak a less dominating language or even a dominated language.

Indeed, it is not always easy to distinguish between a L1 and a L2 because a mother tongue can be forgotten or even lost for many reasons while a second language may become dominant, being a necessity for work and everyday life and therefore sometimes leading to the disappearance of the mother tongue.

The disappearance of languages is not a new phenomenon and is even increasing with the globalization. Indeed, a small number of languages are already dominating the world. However, there is now, all over the world, a new tendency aiming at maintaining and even reviving some minority languages because the importance of the specific heritage of every language is now recognized. That is now the case for many Indigenous languages everywhere in the world.

The following example illustrates that phenomenon.

Example: Cree in Québec

Cree is an Aboriginal language spoken on a vast territory of Canada comprising many provinces. Cree has many varieties that are mutually understandable, although the differences are bigger when the varieties are spoken by very distant communities such as the Chisasibi Cree Nation in Québec and the Enoch Cree Nation in Alberta. Cree can in fact be seen as a continuum of languages that, for some, includes Cree and related languages such as Innu and Naskapi. However, only the Cree communities that are part of Eeyou-Istchee in the James Bay area of Québec and are represented by the Grand Council of the Cree are considered here.

Cree is facing disappearance everywhere in Canada. In Québec, however, the Cree Nations have their own school board, the Cree School Board, that is responsible for providing primary and secondary education for the youth and adult sectors.

Nevertheless, Québec Cree Nations are facing a complex problem because not only are they in an acculturation process, having to find their

---

[10] Those six languages are the official languages of the United Nations Organization.

collective identity and to protect their language by studying it in school, but they also have to learn in school English, the dominant language of Canada and French, the official language of Québec.

Of course, such a situation raises major questions in Cree communities, some people wanting Cree to be taught in school, other people wanting only English and French to be taught in school and other people wanting only English and Cree to be taught in school.

It must also be specified here that there is no standardized way[11] to write Cree, the speakers of the northern variety disagreeing with the speakers of the southern variety. Consequently, there is no written tradition in Cree and the literacy process, one of the main goals of primary education, if done in Cree, cannot lead to the appropriation of thorough knowledge in that language because of the lack of written documents in that language. However, if written Cree is not taught, it could lead, according to some people, to the disappearance of Cree language and culture.

In that context, it is not an easy task to know what the L1 of Cree learners is, especially after a few years in school.

The confusion surrounding their L1 is reflected in the teaching of languages to Cree students provided by their own school board, the Cree School Board. Cree is taught across the curriculum because, in general, it is the language of instruction until grade three of the primary level before being taught as a content matter for the rest of the school program.

In the case of English and French L2, languages of instruction from grade four of the primary level to secondary V (grade 11), there are two programs, French immersion for French (French Language Arts being considered too difficult) and English Language Arts for English. In both cases however, students have to pass either a French L2 or an English L2 exam even though they follow a French immersion program or an English L1 (Language Arts) program. It is not strange, in that context, to have schools giving French L2 or English L2 exams to students who followed a more challenging curriculum, hoping that they will pass the exams and get their high school diploma. That, nevertheless, illustrates the ambiguity found in Cree country around the notions of L1 and L2.

---

[11] The syllabary used to write Cree was invented by James Evans in the 1830s for the Ojibwe and is now used for many Aboriginal languages of Canada.

The same problem may also be found in many Aboriginal communities in Canada and in numerous Indigenous communities all over the world because they are going through a collective identity crisis.

The problematic of Aboriginal languages in Canada can be best understood in the broader context of Canadian language policies in general.

Canada's Official and Aboriginal Languages

In theory, Canada has two official languages, English and French. In practice, however, English is the dominant language almost everywhere in the country except in the province of Québec (outside of Montréal). Even in Montréal, the biggest city in Québec, French is threatened by English and that is the reason why the federal government of Canada presented in February 2021 a white paper that 'presents the Government of Canada's intentions for a reform of official languages and the modernization of the *Official Languages Act* ... (Her Majesty the Queen in Right of Canada, 2021, p. 7)'.

At the provincial level, only Québec has French as the official language while New Brunswick has English and French as official languages and while the eight other provinces are English provinces.

As for the Aboriginal languages, none is an official language of Canada, even though the federal government recognizes that 'Indigenous languages are the first spoken languages of our country (Her Majesty the Queen in Right of Canada, 2021, p. 7)'. *The Indigenous Languages Act* of 2019 (amended in 2020) aims, among other things, 'at support and promote the use of Indigenous languages, including Indigenous sign languages (Government of Canada, 2020, p. 4)'.

Moreover, Canadian Provinces do not recognize any Aboriginal language as an official language. Only two territories (out of three) give an official status to Aboriginal languages, the Nunavut Territory and the Northwest Territories, while the Yukon Territory does not (it recognizes only English and French as official languages). In the Nunavut Territory, the official languages are English, French and two Inuit languages, Inuktitut and Inuinnaqtun while, in the Northwest Territories, the official languages are English, French, Chipewyan, Cree, Gwich'n, Inuktitut, Inuinnaqtun, Inuvialuktun, North Slavey, South Slavey and Tlicho.

The Concept of Culture[12]

The concept of culture is defined according to the more general light of different paradigms in L2 didactics and that is why there are varied definitions of the concept.

For some classical paradigm supporters, culture means the cultural products, more specifically L2 literature or literatures: in English for instance, we can study British, American, Australian, Canadian literatures and so on.

It is important to note here that supporters of this paradigm dominate to these days English L2 teaching in universities, at least in Canada, sometimes creating numerous problems, because many learners come from contexts where this paradigm no longer exists, for example those learners who used a communicative approach at the primary and secondary levels, as it will be seen later.

For supporters of other paradigms, culture refers to the customs of L2 speakers and they will want their learners to know the cuisine, the music and the traditional holydays of L2 speakers.

For the radical paradigm supporters, culture means the specific color the L2 gives to reality and the influence the social context has on the L2. The context and the language are indeed closely interrelated and the result of that symbiotic relation, 'the reality of reality' as Watzlawick (1984) puts it is the culture. Chomsky's (1957) cognitivism, Piaget's (1967) constructivism and Vygotsky's (1978) socio-constructivism also contributed to this new conception of culture that still impacts on L2 didactics.

The following testimony describes how communication can be affected by culture.

Testimony 2: When Culture Blocks Communication

The following event happened in the Chennai area.

"I am in an airport in Southern India, a Tamil country, to deliver a paper on L2 teaching. I have to go to the washroom and as I don't know where it is, I go to a counter where there is a clerk who should be able to help me.

"Good morning Miss. Is the bathroom that way?"

---

[12] In L2 didactics, we can apply Stern's dichotomy between L1 and L2 to cultures and therefore have two sets of cultures, C1 and C2.

The clerk answers with a gentle nodding of the head so characteristic of the Indian Tamil gestures and that is between the sign we use to say yes and the one we use to say no in Canada. I don't know at all if it's a yes or a no. Realizing my confusion, the clerk nods again an finally says: "Yes". I therefore hurry in the direction I indicated. It's at the end of the airport. I arrive at the end and realize that there's nothing. I therefore rush in the other direction and, walking faster this time, I reach the other end of the airport where I finally find the bathroom. I suddenly remember that I was told not to ask, in that area, a yes or no question because the person you are asking the question will always answer yes because answering no would be impolite. The Tamil clerk was being kind to me by answering that the bathroom was in the direction I was pointing even though the bathroom was in fact in the opposite direction."

Culture also has an impact on everyday life as illustrated in the following testimony:

Testimony 3: How Culture Influences Everyday Life

The following event happened in Northern Québec
"*It is the birthday of a Cree colleague and she received a cake for the occasion. It is a big round cake and she is going to cut it. However, contrary to what I was expecting, she does not immediately cut it in individual pieces, but, with the knife, she cuts a circle in the cake and then another circle and then another circle. Then, she gives a piece of that strangely cut cake to everyone. It is amazing, I would have never imagined a cake could be cut that way. I then think that the concept of fractions is probably different for a Cree mind than it is for an Eurocentric mind. Indeed, the cake is for the whole group and the birthday is also everybody's birthday. The colleague told me that she cut the cake the Cree way!*"

Moreover, needless to say that, at least for major international languages such as English, French, Spanish or Arabic, which are spoken by many people from different regions of the world, culture cannot be linked to only one variety of a specific language: for example, we cannot speak of 'the' English culture without being more specific as to the historical, social, political, economic, institutional contexts and so on, because those contexts contribute to the construction of the culture that is constantly evolving.

For the supporters of the radical paradigm, it is not possible to say that a specific way to use a language is superior to another and that, for instance, Paris French is superior to Montreal French, that London English is superior to New York English, that Madrid Spanish is superior to Buenos Aires Spanish, that Lisbon Portuguese is superior to Rio de Janeiro Portuguese.

The Concept of L2 Learner[13]

A L2 learner is somebody learning a L2 in a formal setting as opposed to somebody acquiring a L2 in an informal setting, with friends for example.

The tasks of the learner will, of course, vary according to the paradigm in which the course is given.

In the classical paradigm for instance, students will have to focus on the study and practice of the written language by learning grammar rules and reading literary texts while, in the communicative paradigm, they will focus on the oral language and expository prose reading.

The concept of L2 learner is also related to the concept of L2 teacher and the concept of L2 method and depends on what is given priorities by the paradigm: the language, the method, the student, the teaching or the learning process.

The Concept of L2 Teacher

A L2 teacher is somebody who teaches a L2 in a formal setting, generally a classroom. The L2 the teacher is teaching can be his or her L1, but it is far from always being the case. The task of the L2 teacher will of course vary according to paradigms in which the course is given.

For instance, L2 teachers who support the behaviorist paradigm will use memorization and repetition exercises, while those who support the radical paradigm will use learners' creativity and spontaneity.

The concept of L2 teacher is of course related to the concept of L2 learner and also on the understanding L2 teachers have of the concepts of method, teaching and learning and will be colored by a specific paradigm.

L2 teachers who support the radical paradigm are sometimes called L2 facilitators or guides as in traditional Aboriginal teaching.

---

[13] The term learner is best suited for Aboriginal peoples learning a second language than other terms such as pupil or student, because, as it will be explained later, it more suitably describes the traditional learning process of oral cultures where learning is seen as a lifelong process.

The Concepts of L2 Teaching and Learning

L2 teaching is the process undertaken by L2 teachers, while L2 learning is the process undertaken by L2 learners.

We have to point out here that in order to learn a language, one must be able to understand it, as illustrated by the following testimony.

Testimony 4: Clues that Allow Understanding

The following event happened in the Beijing area.
"I have been trying to watch TV for several days without success because I don't understand a word of what it's said. Programs are in Mandarin, a language I can barely understand except for a few town names. All of a sudden, they show a weather program with small drawings of the sun and clouds. I am finally able to understand that it will be 0 in Beijing, 10 in Shanghai and -20 in Harbin. I was able to understand something only because of small clues and without those clues I would still be in the dark."

As someone learning a L2 must absolutely understand in order to learn, L2 teaching must use meaningful contexts with the learners as we will see later.[14]

As we said earlier, the processes of L2 teaching and L2 learning are different especially when they are colored by two different paradigms.

For instance, as we also mentioned above, students who completed a high school L2 program using a communicative approach may well be disappointed by a university L2 course where the emphasis is put on literature. As a matter of fact, the communicative paradigm coloring a communicative approach (very popular nowadays in Canadian high schools) is totally different from the classical paradigm coloring a literature approach (still prevalent in Canadian universities), because the goals and means of those two paradigms are not the same at all.

As mentioned, since learners can learn a L2 only when exposed to comprehensible data, the teaching process must provide them with meaningful linguistic contexts that allow them to use their background knowledge.[15]

---

[14] Also see Krashen (1981, 1985).
[15] See Demers (1990) for further discussion of that topic.

As noted by Krashen (1982), someone can know the grammar, the rules of a language, without being able to speak the language while someone else can speak a language without knowing the grammar. The conscious process leading to the knowledge of a language grammar is called learning and the unconscious process leading to the use of a language is called acquisition.

Teaching and learning processes are also influenced by the age of learners. Puberty, for instance, is a crucial age in the learning of languages because at that age, learners identify more with a specific linguistic group in order to build their social identity. For example, in English Canada, when native speakers of French reach puberty, they may well start using English among themselves even in the classroom of a French school because they wish to identify with the majority group who speaks English. Among the Québec Cree though, native speakers of Cree reaching puberty may well start using Cree in the classroom because they are proud to be Cree.

The Concept of L2 Method

A L2 method is a set of objectives, rules, techniques, methodologies and exercises organized according to explicit or implicit principles and colored by a specific paradigm.

Methods inspired by the classical, progressivist and behaviorist paradigms focus on form (grammar, pronunciation ...), while methods inspired by communicative and radical paradigms focus on message (communication, meaning ...).

The Concept of L2 Didactics Paradigms

A L2 didactic paradigm is a set of approaches, methods, techniques, exercises and manuals conceptualized by didacticians who want to organize the vast and complex area of L2 teaching.

Indeed, the number of different L2 teaching ways we encounter today on the market is so great, that it is useful to compare those ways and to seek their similarities and differences in order to better understand them.

The paradigms described in this book also exist in other areas of education and even in other areas of humanities and social sciences.

Paradigms have their specific goals and means: explicit grammar teaching and systematic use of translation in order to learn literature for the classical paradigm or intensive oral repetition and memorization in order to perfectly reproduce oral words and sentences for the behaviorist paradigm.

The paradigms contain the factors we just defined, giving them a specific color as illustrated in Fig. 1.

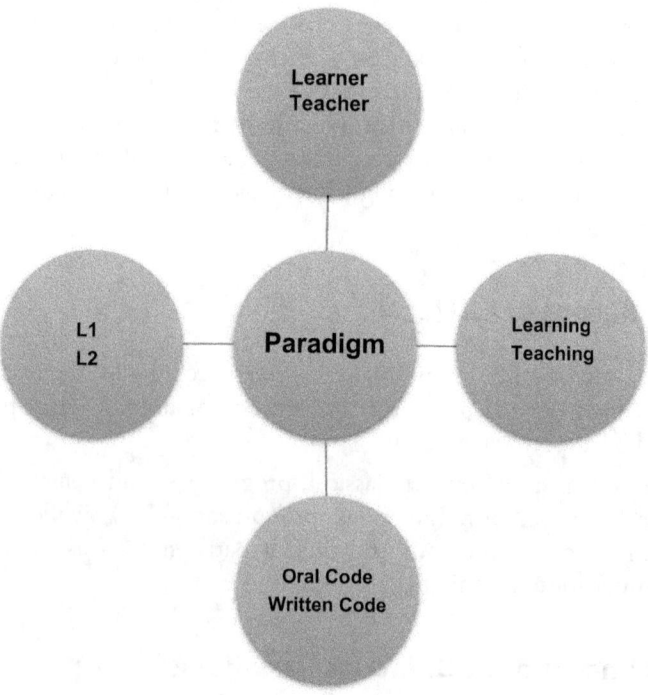

Fig. 1: Constituant Factors of L2 Didactics Paradigms

Chapter 2:
Eurocentric L2 Didactics Paradigms

Historical Aspects

Different authors suggested many models to classify general education practices. Among those authors, there are Houssay (1987), Joyce and Weil (1996) and Bertrand (1998, p. 13) who specifies that:

> It seems necessary to classify education theories because their great numbers do not help their comprehension or the orientation choice ... Of course, there are different ways of categorising the discourses and practices in education.

In L2 didactics, we can also distinguish a number of paradigms or major trends such as those suggested by Stern (1984), Bess (1992) and Caravolas (1994). Demers, Pardo and Pelletier (2006) also suggested L2 didactic paradigms based on Elias and Merriam's (1983) adult education paradigms.

The main paradigms described in this book are the classical, the progressivist, the behaviorist, the communicative and the radical paradigms. For every paradigm, there is a specific type of methods: the grammar-translation method for the classical paradigm, the direct method for the progressivist paradigm, the structural method for the behaviorist paradigm, the communicative method for the communicative paradigm and the accelerated method for the radical paradigms. All the paradigms inspire methods that are used today in L2 teaching and learning.

The classical paradigm is the oldest[16] one since it goes back to Antiquity. Indeed, in those days, many students from remote areas attended universities giving courses in a language the students had to learn. For

---

[16] There are also various "natural" approaches to L2 teaching and learning but they do not belong to our classification because they are not used in a formal setting. As a

example, in the fifth century before our era, the ancient University of Taxila in the Indian subcontinent used Sanskrit as the medium of instruction and, in the fourth century of our era, the University of Constantinople used Greek while, in the tenth century of our era, the University of al-Azhar in Cairo used Arabic. In the first European universities in the twelfth century of our era, the language of instruction was Latin.

In fact, the classical paradigm is more than Eurocentric, since it is deeply related to the discovery of writing in many civilizations: China, India, Persia, Greece, Rome and Egypt, for example.

The major goal of that paradigm is to have the students read the classical texts of the dominant languages.

The classical paradigm is still largely used today in higher education institutions worldwide.

Figure 2 illustrates the extensive use of the classical paradigm.

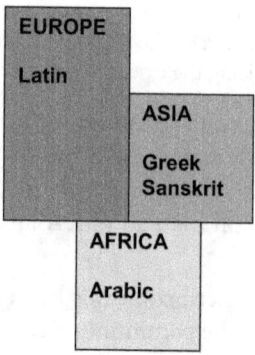

Fig. 2: Extent of the Classical Paradigm

The progressivist paradigm goes back to industrialization and the invention of the *International Phonetic Alphabet* (IPA) in the nineteenth century. This paradigm can be seen as a reaction to the classical paradigm. Indeed, the progressivist paradigm puts the emphasis on the oral component of the language. However, as it was mainly used with adult learners and generally requires native speakers to teach their own language, it was

---

matter of fact, L2 languages have been learned since times immemorial: Australian Aboriginals have been multilingual for thousands of years.

not as widely used as other paradigm.[17] It is nevertheless still used today, mainly by private language schools and self-education methods.

The behaviorist paradigm goes back to the early 1950s and is still in use today.

The major goal of those two paradigms is to get the students to master the oral language. The latter is based on behaviorist psychology and structural linguistics.[18]

The communicative paradigm goes back to the late 1960s and is used today by people who want to be able to understand and speak a L2.

The radical paradigm goes back to the middle of the 1970s.

Those two paradigms aim at students' autonomy, but the radical paradigm also aims at students' creativity so that students are able to transfer their L2 knowledge to diverse contexts. The communicative paradigm is based on humanistic psychology and constructivism, while the radical paradigm is based on transpersonal psychology and new communication theory.

It is important to specify here that for the radical paradigm, it is not possible to teach a language without teaching the culture related to that language because, according to that paradigm, a language is not only a communication tool but also a specific way of seeing the world or even a specific way of being.

Often, in that paradigm, the teacher makes sure that learners know the gestures, the proxemics and the notion of time specific to the language taught because, as seen before, these factors are important in the communication process. Here are examples:

1. French speakers and Spanish speakers generally make more gestures and touch one another more when they talk among themselves than English speakers and German speakers do when they talk among themselves.
2. The distance there is between two people engaged in a conversation is in general smaller between Arabic speakers and Mandarin speakers when they talk among themselves than the distance there is between Japanese speakers when they talk among themselves.

---

[17] See Berlitz (1897).
[18] See Lado (1964) and Skinner (1957).

3. The notion of time for Spanish and Arabic speakers is more cyclical than the notion of time for English and Japanese speakers, which is more linear.

Many methods are based on more than one Eurocentric paradigms: for example, the multidimensional curriculum for French L2 teaching proposed by Leblanc (1990) for Core French in Canadian high schools is based on classical and communicative paradigms, while the methods used by the Canada School of Public Service to teach languages to public servants are also based on more than one paradigm: the behaviorist and the communicative paradigms.

Table 1 summarizes the approximate dates of the rising of the paradigms in the history of L2 didactics.

Tab. 1: Approximate Dates of the Rising of Eurocentric Paradigms in L2 Didactics History

-500	Classical
1850	Progressivist
1950	Behaviorist
1965	Communicative
1975	Radical

Pedagogical Aspects

When L2 didacticians realized that the classical and the behaviorist paradigms were not efficient in teaching languages for communication purposes, they had to look at alternatives to linguistics, such as sociolinguistics[19] and pragmatics.[20] As a matter of fact, both classical and behaviorist paradigms focus on the study of the language itself and not on its use. That is why teachers and learners knew rules and words of the L2 without being able to use it for oral communication.

The communicative paradigm started in Canada in 1965 with the French immersion programs for English speaking learners. In a French

---

[19] The study of a languages in relation to social factors.
[20] The branch of linguistics dealing with language in use and the contexts in which it is used.

immersion program, teachers and learners use the L2 to teach content and, therefore, both teachers and learners communicate in the L2. By contrast, in a regular French program, grammar and words are studied, but French is not used as a communication tool, because it is taught as a subject matter.

In the late 1970s, when it was realized that L2 teaching methods used in regular programs did not prepare the learners to properly master the L2 oral components, (something that immersion programs could achieve), L2 didacticians and L2 teachers had to abandon their methods. Since their methods were based on the psychological trend of behaviorism and the linguistic trend of structuralism and, because there did not seem to exist an adequate theoretical framework for L2 teaching and learning, there was a long period of trial and error and, quite frankly, many L2 teachers were confused and looking for new ways to help learners master the oral component of the L2. Indeed, Germain (1993, p. V) even states the following[21]:

> It is not easy to define what the communicative approach is. Indeed, there is not ONE communicative approach but many conceptions or interpretations of what the communicative approach is. And the authors seem to agree more on what IT IS NOT than on what it is: an approach that aims at having the pupils communicate efficiently in a second or foreign language.

It was then almost impossible to define what the communicative approach was, since many researchers and teachers in the field were trying various techniques, often with no real results.

In the middle of the 1980s, *The Canadian Association of Second Language Teachers* launched a national study whose goal was to elaborate an effective communicative approach to L2 teaching and learning for regular French L2 programs. Indeed, this was an important endeavor, which would propose a method that would enable English Canadians to become competent in French. Immersion programs were producing bilingual learners, but the regular French programs were not. Leblanc (1990) published a synthesis of the research containing 92 conclusions and a multidimensional curriculum composed of four syllabi, including a cultural syllabus and a communicative-experiential syllabus (Tremblay, R., M. Duplantie and D. Huot, 1999). In a communicative-experiential

---

[21] All the French texts are translated in English by the author.

syllabus, learners are the focus of the communicative activities and they are asked to speak about something that is motivating and familiar to them. That syllabus inspired what was first called intensive French and is now called the neurolinguistics approach to language teaching and learning.

Nowadays, there are various methods that focus on communication: among them, there are the action-oriented approach, the neurolinguistics approach and the radical approach.

The Action-Oriented Approach

In *Le Conseil de l'Europe* (2019, p. 15), the action-oriented approach considers 'the users and learners of a language as social actors having tasks to accomplish'. That is the reason why the tasks to be completed have to be accomplished in a context that is meaningful for the learners.

Kwadzo (2016, p. 80) even specifies that, in the action-oriented approach:

> It is worth noticing that the accomplishment of the tasks must be situated in a social context that is pertinent to the learner: this context allows the learner as a person to identify and realise her or his learning projects. It is by situating this task realisation goal and pertinent projects in the learner's life in relation with the learner's context that her or his learning will be meaningful.

The focus being on a task to be accomplished by the learners, the approach uses the L2 in a meaningful fashion. In that sense, it is similar to the French immersion programs. The action-oriented approach focuses more on the use of the language than on the study of the language itself (Puren, 2007).

The Neurolinguistics Approach

Created from the communicative-experiential syllabus previously mentioned, the neurolinguistics approach of Netten and Germain (2012) is based on the fact that there are two kinds of memory: the declarative or explicit memory and the procedural or implicit memory.

In L2 teaching and learning, the declarative memory is responsible for the memorization of grammar rules and words, while the procedural memory is responsible for the acquisition of linguistic reflexes. It is important to know that there is no direct relation between the two types of memory and that grammar rules and words learned through the declarative memory will not be acquired by the procedural memory. That is the reason why teaching L2 grammar rules and lists of words will not be useful for the fluent use of the L2.

As mentioned earlier, Krashen (1981) already made a distinction between L2 learning and L2 acquisition: L2 learning leads to the knowledge of grammar and words and L2 acquisition leads to the mastery of the language. However, it is only later that a psychological framework was described to explain differences between the two kinds of memory (Paradis, 2009).

In this approach, the focus is on the use of the oral language by the learners and the activities have to be motivating and close to the needs of the learners.

The Radical Approach[22]

This approach is related to two main theoretical frameworks: the new communication (Winkin, 2014)[23] and the transpersonal psychology (Grof, 2000).[24] According to those frameworks, communication is a holistic process that involves all aspects of human beings, including the spiritual aspect.

In this approach, it is critical to create both a good and trustful relationship between the teacher and the learners and a pleasant and relaxed classroom atmosphere. Demers (2008, pp. 52–53) specifies that:

> In the radical paradigm, L2 teachers want their students to be open to the specific world view, the L2 culture in the broadest sense and also to tap

---

[22] That last L2 didactics approach is classified as radical because it aims at creativity and empowerment of the person, a goal that is shared by Freire's approach to literacy and classified as radical by Elias and Merriam (1983).

[23] As mentioned earlier, the new communication theory suggests a way to classify languages that differ from what is proposed by traditional linguistics which classifies languages in groups and families. For example, speakers of a language may use more gestures when they speak than speakers of another language. Gestures, proximity, eye contacts, touching and conception of time can be used to classify languages (see Hall, 1959, 1966, Birdwhistell, 1960, for further details).

[24] Lozanov (1978) uses baroque music to improve the memorisation process of L2 acquisition because this allows the two hemispheres of the brain to function together.

on their unused full potential, knowledge and skills, something that can be achieved by using diverse means such as music and imagination ...

One of the objectives of the radical approach is to address both hemispheres of the brain to help the acquisition of the L2. Using the L2 will involve the left hemisphere of the brain, because the language center is essentially located in the left hemisphere. As for the right hemisphere, that can be done by using diverse techniques such as listening to baroque music, using gestures, relaxing, dreaming, etc.

For example, the author of the *Accelerative Integrated Method* (AIM), Wendy Maxwell, explains why her method works (Maxwell, 2014, p. 3)[25]:

> Through this approach, all target vocabulary to be acquired by the student is taught kinaesthetically, visually and in an auditory manner, thus responding to a variety of learning styles. Because words are kinaesthetically presented through gesture, and contextualized through story and drama, students learn to see and feel the language.

The action-oriented approach, the neurolinguistics approach and the radical approach are very widely used in Canada today and could even be complementary since they are all in the communicative paradigm or, as Rousse-Malpat (2019, p. 79) says:

> The most important principle of these methods is to provide lots of meaningful L2 exposure and use in the L2 classroom. To achieve that goal, teachers and learners only use the target language in the classroom from day one and focus on providing input and scaffolding the output, from pure repetition to use and reuse of chunks present in the input. To do so, a lot of attention is put on oral skills and in a later stage on writing skills.

---

[25] The gestures imply the use of the right hemisphere of the brain.

Chapter 3:
Descriptions of Eurocentric L2 Didactics Paradigms

The Classical Paradigm

The main goal of L2 teaching in the classical paradigm is to enable students to read important authors, writers and philosophers of a specific language in that language. The oral language is not considered important and therefore not taught. Some students however, for example the French writer Montaigne, succeeded in mastering the oral code of the L2 before taking courses in that paradigm by hiring private teachers.

The L2 teacher explains the grammar rules and provides the students with written exercises and vocabulary lists. The students have to translate texts written in L2 in their L1 (this exercise is called a version) and texts written in their L1 in L2 (this exercise is called a theme).

Students use a L2 grammar book in which the explanations are given in the students' L1, bilingual dictionaries for themes and versions and texts written in L2. Students are expected to have a thorough knowledge of the L2 grammar much more than of the L2 itself.

As seen before, that way of L2 teaching is the oldest one and also one of the most popular, having been used to teach Latin, Greek, Arabic, Sanskrit and Mandarin among others.[26] It should also be underlined here that grammar has always been an interesting research field for scholars: the first grammar known to this day is a grammar of Sanskrit written

---

[26] Interestingly, all those languages are associated with a major religion: Latin with Western Christianity, Greek with Eastern Christianity, Arabic with Islam, Sanskrit with Hinduism and Mandarin with Buddhism.

by Panini, a professor at the ancient University of Taxila, many centuries before our era.

Even today, as already mentioned, the classical paradigm is still very popular especially in higher education, even though it does not teach the oral language.

The following testimony illustrates the classical paradigm.

Testimony 5: The Latin Homework

The following event happened in the Montréal area.

" 'Quousque tandem abutere, Catilina, patienta nostra? ... '

I have been struggling on my Latin version for more than an hour without much success. The Latin-English dictionary is useful but not enough because I don't seem to be able to grasp the spirit of the language that would make me really understand. My translations are too literal and I am not successful in expressing in English the specific meaning of the Latin text. I am constantly asking myself why we spend so much time learning a language that only a few prelates from The Vatican still use. I am not at all convinced that this intellectual exercise will give me anything in the end. It seems to me that it would be much more useful for us to learn Spanish or Italian that come from Latin and are still much in use.

Later, I finally learned that what Cicero wrote means: 'How long, o Catiline, will you abuse our patience?'"

Typical Teaching Procedures for a Classical Lesson

1. The L2 teacher explains in L1 the L2 grammar rules;
2. L2 students ask in L1 questions on the L2 grammar rules;
3. The L2 teacher gives written exercises on the grammar rules and a text to be translated;
4. The students do the exercises and the translation on an individual basis;
5. After a fixed period of time, the L2 teacher collects the students' works;
6. At the beginning of the next lesson, the L2 teacher gives back the students their works that have been corrected and, most of the time, marked.

The Progressivist Paradigm

As the classical paradigm does not teach the oral language, it does not address the needs of those who want to be able to speak a L2. As many immigrant people, during the industrial revolution, needed to speak a L2, a new trend raised in L2 didactics, the progressivist paradigm: the main goal of that paradigm is to have the students learn the oral language. In order to answer people's need for oral competency, Maximilian Berlitz founded a language school in 1878 in Providence, Rhodes Island, and his employee, Nicholas Joly, used only the L2 to teach his courses in a direct way.

Many language schools, using a direct approach, opened their doors to adult learners and some of them are still very popular today as already mentioned.

In that paradigm, the L2 teacher uses the L2 all the time. Students are asked to repeat words and sentences and the teacher corrects their pronunciation and their speech. At the beginning of the course, words and structures are very simple and gradually become more complex. For example, at the beginning of the course, the teacher can give the words and sentences necessary to describe the classroom: by doing so, the teacher provides the students with the clues they need to understand those simple words and sentences and are then able to learn them.

Words and sentences can be grouped under themes: for example, the classroom, the human body, the animals and so on.

Students must repeat and memorize words and sentences. The written language is very rarely used and, when used, it is to help memorizing words and sentences.

The progressivist paradigm emerged in reaction to the classical paradigm and, because of that, it is the opposite of the classical paradigm, as the following testimony illustrates.

Testimony 6: A Night Course in L2

The following event happened in the Montréal area.

"As I want to improve my oral French and because our professor at the college keeps on teaching Baudelaire although a vast majority of students cannot understand most of the texts, I decide to take a French night course.

The night course teacher always uses French in the classroom and, because we are advanced learners, we talk about varied topics of interest.

Finally, I can practice my French and I keep on wandering why our college professor keeps on refusing to practice oral French. Maybe he doesn't speak it well enough."

Typical Teaching Procedures for a Progressivist Lesson

1. The teacher points at various objects in the classroom and say the L2 words for those objects;
2. Every student in the classroom repeats the words;
3. With every word, the teacher makes simple sentences, using the oral language only;
4. Students make simple oral sentences with every word;
5. The teacher makes more complex sentences with every word, using the oral language only;
6. Students make more complex sentences with every word.

The Behaviorist Paradigm

Although the progressivist paradigm focused on the oral language, it is only in the middle of the twentieth century of our era that the oral language was to be taught in public schools. Indeed, at that time, two important research trends were emerging, behaviorist psychology and structural linguistics. Moreover, it then became possible to reproduce the human voice in the classroom with the use of a new technology, the tape recorder.

For structural linguists, the oral language is much more important than the written language while for behaviorist psychologists, the learning process is a set of stimuli and responses. By combining those two disciplines, researchers established the theoretical frame of the structure-behaviorist methods. According to those methods, the oral language has to be taught using appropriate responses to verbal stimuli.

The L2 teacher starts by presenting a new structure, tries to explain its meaning to the students without ever using their L1, asks the students to repeat the structure, corrects their pronunciation, asks them to memorize the structure, to use it in a specific linguistic environment and then, if possible, in a broader context.

The students have to try to understand the new L2 structures, repeat them as well as they can, memorize them and then use them.

The following testimony illustrates this procedure.

Testimony 7: My Students Repeat and Repeat

The following event happened in the Montréal area.

"*'Repeat after me: I am, you are, he is, she is, we are, you are, they are … I am a man, you are a man, he is a man …'*

I teach English as a second language in a high school and I have been asking my students to repeat and keep on repeating the same sentences for over fifteen minutes now and they seem to enjoy it. I start with group repetitions and then I ask every student to repeat in order for me to listen to and correct their pronunciation. The group repetitions go well but, when it comes to individual repetitions, the group becomes noisy."

Even though the behaviorist paradigm is not as popular today as it was from the fifties to the seventies, the L2 methods it promotes are still used today under its new computerized form, computer technology having in fact a very important impact on L2 teaching and learning as it will be explained later.

L2 methods based on the behaviorist paradigm are easy to use by the teacher in the classroom and also in their computerized forms by students wishing to learn a L2 by themselves.[27] It also provides the teacher with excellent pronunciation techniques such as the verbotonal method

Typical Teaching Procedures for a Behaviorist Lesson

1. Study of the L2 phonetics;
2. Introduction of oral L2 structures by the L2 teacher;
3. Repetition and memorization exercises (drills and pattern practice) by the students;
4. Correction by the L2 teacher of the students' speech;
5. Contextualization of the structures;
6. Reading simple texts aloud by the teacher and then the students;

---

[27] The progressivist paradigm also inspired self-learning L2 methods as already mentioned.

7. Correction by the teacher of the students' pronunciation;
8. Written exercises to facilitate the memorization of the structures.

The Communicative Paradigm

The major goal of the communicative paradigm is to allow students to use their L2 in a spontaneous way without having to rely all the time on the specific structures learned in class. As a matter of fact, two research areas inspire the communicative paradigm: humanistic psychology and cognitive psychology.

Indeed, although the emphasis is put on the oral language in the behaviorist paradigm, most of the time, students do not master their L2 well enough to be able to use it outside the classroom. The emphasis is put on the oral form rather than on the communication of a message.

Of course, there are more than one way to put the emphasis on the message as the two following testimonies illustrate.

Testimony 8: I Use a Linguistic Code with my Students

The following event happened in the Montréal area.

"I teach French L2 in an elementary school and use a set of symbols, a code I developed for my students. I use those symbols to write on the blackboard short sentences they can understand. I find that, that way, they do not translate, they speak faster and they are more motivated. The sentences I write are simple: 'the elephant is in the forest, the dog is walking on the sidewalk, the cat catches a mouse.' And my students are finally starting to speak. The school principal comes to my class to evaluate my teaching and, when the lesson is over, he tells me that, in the education courses he took at the university, he never learned the 'linguistic code technique' I use. I don't dare telling him I never learned this code at the university. I enjoy using that technique with my pupils and I like to have fun with the children."

Testimony 9: My L2 Class is Noisy

The following event happened in the Montréal area.

"I teach French L2 in an elementary school. An education consultant comes to see me teach after having asked me if she could do that. After the class, she tells me she is very happy with my teaching and asks me if I would allow another French L2 teacher to come to my class to see how I work. I agree.

> When the other teacher comes, she is stunned: the pupils play all sorts of games, the only rule being that they speak French all the time during the whole 30 minutes of the lesson. In my group, a few children already master their L2 quite well and other students learn by playing with them. As everybody speaks, the class is noisy and because everybody plays, one might think that my pupils lack discipline. Of course, it is not the case, but the other French L2 teacher seems puzzled, because she is used to quiet groups. She must think that I am crazy and that the education consultant is also crazy to have told her to go see such a crazy teacher teach."

Moreover, L2 teachers applying the principles of humanistic and cognitive psychologies focus more on their students' needs and the creative dimension of language than they do on the linguistic code and predictable answers to verbal stimuli. Indeed, a language is first and foremost a highly flexible communication tool. Many L2 learners were already asking for such a change of focus as illustrated by the following testimony.

Testimony 10: My Students Ask me to Change my Teaching Method

> *The following event happened in Northern Ontario.*
> "A student asks me: 'Why don't we do what we did yesterday?'
> 'Because we are following the method.'
> 'Why are we following the method? What we did yesterday was more interesting and we were learning more that way.'
> I teach an intensive French L2 course in a university and, in the method we use, a structural method, there is a part that allows students to speak more freely and, because they are advanced students, they use that part of the method to have fun and use everything they know in French. This part of the method is therefore much more interesting than other parts of the method. As I also noticed that students learn from one another French words and expressions, I agree to help them do what they want (and need), at least on an experimental basis, and allow them to speak more, even though they may make more mistakes.
> After that "experiment" my courses were never the same: without knowing it, I had just tried, for the first time in my life and before the communicative approach had become popular, the communicative paradigm. I just could not go back to the behaviorist paradigm, at least with intermediate or more advanced learners."

In the communicative paradigm, students practice their oral L2 and read and study L2 authentic documents, expository prose texts written for L1 readers and carrying information about specific topics. Literary texts are not excluded but, as already mentioned, this paradigm focuses on the use of the L2 as a communication tool. As the emphasis is put on the message rather than on the form, the results are sometimes rather surprising as they can go far beyond the classroom, as illustrated by the following testimony.

Testimony 11: I Discover the Impact of Communication in a L2

The following event happened in the Montréal area.

"In a college L2 course I was giving, I had put a lot of emphasis on communication and we had had many interesting conversations on different topics.

The last day of the course, two of my students came to see me together to tell me how much they liked the course. As they seemed to know each other quite well, I asked for how long they had known each other. They told me that they had been working together for more than twenty years but that they had begun to know each other only at the beginning of the course because the course had given them a chance to speak to each other, to listen to one another, to understand each other and to become friends.

They made my day, that time. I had my students practice communication in that course as the humanist paradigm wants L2 teachers to do and that practice had impacts that went far beyond the classroom. I knew it was for the best".

Typical Teaching Procedures for a Communicative Lesson

There are no real typical procedures in that paradigm. As a matter of fact, as teachers focus on students' needs and the use of authentic documents, most of the time they have to find and even create their own teaching material. That situation can create problems for L2 teachers, as they sometimes may have to devote a lot of time to the preparation of their lessons. That situation can even be seen as a limit of the communicative paradigm. The suggested procedures are therefore given only as examples of what could be done.

1. The L2 teachers reads an authentic document aloud;
2. In L2, the teacher explains words and sentences students do not understand;
3. The teacher proposes communicative activities that allow students to practice their L2;
4. Students do the suggested activities in small groups;
5. A student in each group tells the whole class what his or her group did;
6. The other students listen to the student who speaks.

The Immersion Programs

French immersion programs are very popular and they belong to the communicative paradigm because the goal of those programs is to teach French L2 in an indirect fashion, by using students L2 as a means to teach them other school subjects.

Numerous articles and books are written on French immersion programs (e.g., Mannavarayan, 2002, Rebuffot, 1993) and there are now French immersion programs across Canada and also immersion programs for other languages in several countries and the popularity of immersion is still growing.

The first immersion program, a French immersion program, started in St-Lambert, a rich English community on the south shore of the St-Lawrence River, near Montreal in 1965. The new program was created to answer the needs of Anglophone students who wanted to learn French, but could not do so with their traditional Core French program that was based on the classical paradigm and also, to a lesser degree, on the behaviorist paradigm. That new immersion program was in fact based on the communicative paradigm, even though very few people had realized that at the time because the new paradigm was just beginning.

The conclusions of Lambert and Tucker (1972), two professors from McGill University in Montreal who initiated what was then called the St-Lambert experiment, were not only that the immersion students were able to use French to a much greater degree than the Core French students but also that their knowledge of other school matters was as good as the one of the Core French students. That is the reason why immersion programs became so popular. Students could keep on learning content matters while learning French L2.

French immersion programs started to diversify: early and late immersions, submersion, total and partial immersions and so on and their popularity became so great that it created many controversies, some researchers such as Hammerly (1989) even arguing that the programs were too expensive and that, because of them, many English speaking teachers could not find a job anymore, school boards across Canada having started to hire French speaking teachers.

Much research was and still is devoted to immersion. One of the conclusions of that research is that French immersion students speak 'immersion French', a new variety of French highly influenced by English on the phonetic, syntactic and lexical levels.

Another consequence of the French immersion programs is the great difficulty it created for many French departments in English universities in Canada. Those departments were (and still are in many instances) giving French L2 courses based on the classical paradigm to students who now came from high schools that were giving French L2 course based on the communicative paradigm. Indeed, the classical paradigm was no longer relevant, and English universities were not answering students' needs and, in many instances, are still not.

In fact, French L2 courses given by French departments in many English universities are designed for French L1 learners wanting to study literature and not for French L2 learners wishing to improve and practice their L2 and are simply too difficult for L2 learners.

French immersion programs' popularity demonstrates that the birth of a new paradigm threatens the existing educational institutions' infrastructures and is not welcomed by the supporters of the older paradigm who do not want to change even for the best. That is of course the case not only in L2 didactics, but in many other areas also.

Nevertheless, the popularity of immersion programs is still growing all over the world.

The Radical Paradigm

As already mentioned, two research areas provide basis for the radical paradigm: transpersonal psychology that originated at the Esalen Centre near Big Sur in California and the new communication theory which is also called the Palo Alto School because it originated at the psychiatric hospital of Palo Alto, also in California.

In the radical paradigm, L2 teachers want their learners to be opened to the specific world view, the L2 culture in the broadest meaning and also to tap on their often unused full potential, knowledge and skills, something teachers can do by using diverse means such as music and imagination, as illustrated by the following testimonies.

Testimony 12: My Students Listen to Baroque Music

The following event happened in the Montréal area.
"We are in an elementary school where I teach French L2. I dim the light while the pupils listen to baroque music. I tell them to imagine a story they will then draw and tell the others. Noisy a few minutes ago, the group is now quiet and a few younger children even fell asleep."

Testimony 13: My Students Are Dreaming

The following event happened in the Montréal area.
"We are in a college were I give a L2 course. My students, eyes closed, are relaxing in their chair. I ask them to imagine they are taking a walk in a forest and to visualize their walk as well as they can for a few minutes. I then ask them to open their eyes and, one after another, they tell everybody their directed dream. That way, I allow them to think directly in their L2, without using their L1, to increase their vocabulary and to use their imagination, a major factor in L2 learning. Moreover, they are not afraid of making mistakes and therefore speak easily when telling the others their dream."

This apparently new paradigm is in fact a very old one even though it is still not well known.

Indeed, a very long time ago, Indian educators, in what they still call the Guru Tradition,[28] used only the oral language in their teaching, even forbidding the use of the written language, convinced that writing encouraged laziness, and developed highly efficient memorization techniques allowing the memorization of extremely long texts. In India, there are still Hindu monks, Brahmans, who are able to memorize the hundred thousands of verses of the Vedas, Hindu holy scriptures: some spend their entire life reciting the verses in order to be able to remember every single one of them in the event of a catastrophe that would kill most of humankind and destroy the sacred written texts.

As Drury (1981, p. 15) points out, the pioneers of the human potential movement and, more specifically, transpersonal psychology, one of the two components of the radical paradigm, are related to psychoanalysis:

> There is no doubt that both the Human Potential Movement and the New Age alike have been strongly influenced by such thinkers

---

[28] See Pujyasri (1991).

as William James, Sigmund Freud, Carl Jung, Alfred Adler and Wilhelm Reich.

To those first authors, we must add Maslow, Sutich, Perls, Barber, Tart and Groff. Groff was the first one to use the terms transpersonal psychology to describe this new trend in the field of psychology in the sixties of the last century: the new trend was considered by many as a fourth trend in psychology along with psychoanalysis, behaviorist psychology and humanistic psychology.

Transpersonal psychology aims at exploring the realm of human consciousness and, in order to do that, it uses religious or mystic practices of different religious traditions and altered states of consciousness.[29] Highly criticized at first, transpersonal psychology is now recognized, taught in many universities and used by several educators, psychologists and practitioners.

As that new trend was developing in the psychological field mainly at the Esalen Centre where most of the authors we mentioned earlier stayed and worked, the Palo Alto school[30] was also developing another trend with researchers such as Bateson, Beavin, Birdwhistell, Hall, Jackson, Mead and Wastlawick: this new trend in communication studies would change, in a radical fashion, the concepts of language and culture. For that trend, language and culture are linked in an intrinsic fashion, influencing one another in such a way that they cannot be separated and, combined, provide a perception of reality, specific to every language and culture.

As a matter of fact, when a child is born, he or she is immediately submersed in a linguistic and cultural world that he or she must absolutely grasp to survive. Language is imposed on him or her with its particular sounds and signs and specific interpretation of the world that he or she will keep forever. For instance, if a language has only three words to describe all the colors of the spectrum, the infant will have only those three words to describe all the perceived colors. The infant will also gradually become incapable to perceive language sounds that are not used in its language, that are not phonemes in its L1.

---

[29] See Groff (1992) and Tart (1990).
[30] The school, also called the Invisible College because its authors were not located at a specific institution but rather coming from different institutions and fields, proposes a new way to understand human communication, much broader than traditional linguistics and sociolinguistics..

The culture will also be imposed on the infant with its rule, regulations, restrictions, taboos, music, traditions and religion as the following testimonies illustrate.

Testimony 14: My Religion Blinds me

The following event happened in the Montréal area.
"When I was a kid, the catholic brothers would bring us to church to confess on a regular basis, at least once a month. As it was considered a sin not to confess any sin, I had to think a lot to find one and, after much introspection and thought, I had finally found one that was very useful because it could mean almost anything. I would always tell the priest that I had disobeyed my parents. The priests never asked me any question and I did not have to give any explanation. The priests must have thought that we were all very bad kids because every one of us would tell the same sin as I later realized that my idea of a sin was a very popular one. We had to go to confession and we would have never have thought that there could have been another way to live. We were all Roman Catholics and our culture was full of religious symbols, prayers and ceremonies and we could not even imagine that there could have been anything else because doing that would have been a mortal sin and we could go to hell. It is only later in my life that I realized that there was indeed something else."

Testimony 15: Being Sick in an Alien Language

The following event happened in the Beijing area.
"January 1985: I work in Beijing, PRC, as a foreign expert and one morning, I wake up with a sore throat and a fever.
I go to the nearest clinic and try to tell the doctor who examines me what I have. I use every language I know without success because she speaks Mandarin only, a language I don't know at all. I then decide to use gestures to try to explain what I have, but the doctor still does not understand because Chinese gestures are different. She decides to take my blood pressure over my winter coat. I try to take off my coat but the doctor does not want me to do that and gets upset.
Her reaction upsets me, but I decide to let her proceed.
While taking my blood pressure over my coat, she finally realizes I have a fever and understands I also have a sore throat. She writes a prescription, gives it to me and points in the direction of what could be a dispensary.
The prescription is of course written in Chinese by a Chinese doctor and I cannot read it. The doctor takes a small sheet, writes $60 \times 3 \times 10$ on the sheet, gives it to me and, pointing at the number 10, she utters a word that sounds like "days". As I finally realize or think I realize I have to take 1800 pills in 10 days, I get really scared. I must be a lot sicker than I thought I was.

Nevertheless, I go to what could be a pharmacy as I thought she indicated. I give the prescription to the apothecary (he most certainly does not look like a pharmacist to me). The apothecary takes the prescription and disappears. He comes back a few minutes later and gives me 30 minuscule bottles each containing 60 almost microscopic capsules of a traditional Chinese medication I do not know anything about."

Testimony 16: My Students' Culture Blocks their L2 Acquisition

The following event happened in the Vancouver area.
"*I give a course to young Japanese women who are L2 beginners. Since the beginning of the course, over a week ago, they do not look at me when they speak to me or when I speak to them. As in the L2 I teach it is crucial to look at the person you speak to or who speaks to you in order for communication to take place, I finally succeed in making them understand that you have to look at the person you speak to or who speaks to you in the L2 they want to learn. Reluctantly, they accept to do that but with great uneasiness: in Japanese, for a young woman to look at a male teacher is considered very impolite and even provocative."*

Testimony 17: A House That Does Not Look Like a House

The following event happened in the Montréal area.
"*I teach a L2 at the elementary level and my students come from many countries.*
I ask them to draw a picture of a house. A few minutes later, a few pupils are proud to show me their picture. What some of them show me does not look like a house at all but more like a plain board with long legs. I tell them that what they drew is not a house and ask them to draw another picture of a real house this time. One of them, although very young, seems to understand that I do not understand and succeeds in explaining to me that, in his country, many people live in pile dwellings. I understand my mistake and tell my pupils that I was wrong and that they drew real houses. They smile at me and keep on drawing."

It is clear from the above testimonies that a culture shapes a specific view of the world to the extent that we can even say that it is a construction of the world and that, for those individuals who belong to that culture, it is the world. At least that is the way new communication supporters see what a culture is.

That is why a L2 cannot be effectively used if not in accordance with its culture and to which it is very closely linked as was said earlier. As an example, Cyrulnik (2000, pp. 44–45) uses greeting rituals:

Greeting rituals are numerous and take very different forms according to the culture ... Hindus cross their hands and lower their head as if they were praying, Arabs touch their heart, mouth and forehead, Americans use their hands as a windshield washer.

The radical paradigm is also based on new communication theory because it is not possible for transpersonal psychology on which it is also based not to take into account the cultural dimension of human beings, one of their most important ones.

Indeed, the human potential movement intends to help individuals use their full potential to accomplish their most important goals. When applied to education and more specifically to L2 teaching and learning, that paradigm puts the emphasis on the person in a way similar to those of Knowles' (1980) andragogy and Freire's (1996) radical pedagogy: learning becomes more important that teaching, learners become more important than teachers and the teachers' role is to facilitate learners' learning process.

Moreover, in certain favorable circumstances, learners can reach results superior to those that can usually be expected from them. To crate those favorable circumstances, authors propose different procedures: Dufeu (1994) proposes theater techniques, Galisson (1983), Lerède (1983) and Lozanov (1978) the use of suggestion, Demers (1995) and Hammerman (1979) the use of hypnosis, Guiora et al. (1980) and Schumann et al. (1978) the use of substances and Dortu (1986) the use of imagination techniques. Whatever the technique used, the results is the creation of an altered state of consciousness in the learners that will allow them to function on a level that differs from the one they are used to and in which their performances are enhanced.

An altered state of consciousness is different from the waking state. We all experience altered states of consciousness when we go to sleep, dream and wake up. Those altered states of consciousness do not have to be induced.

Some people also experience induced altered states of consciousness by meditation and trances for instance. In fact, everyone can be trained with specific techniques to induce altered states of consciousness at will. Most major religious traditions allow and even encourage specific altered states of consciousness induced by prayer, meditation and contemplation: Christian mysticism, Judaic kabala, Muslim sufism, Hindu yoga, Buddhist meditation ... Even shamanist traditions often use natural psychotropic substances, drums, music, chant, and dance to induce altered states of consciousness.

The specific altered states of consciousness used in education by the human potential movement and, more specifically by the L2 didactic radical paradigm, are those that can enhance performances of L2 learners by improving concentration, memory, motivation, imagination or self-esteem, by lowering anxiety or stress, all factors that have a deep impact on L2 learning.

As mentioned earlier, hypnosis induces altered states of consciousness as illustrated in the following testimony.

Testimony 18: Students under Hypnosis

The following event happened in the Vancouver area.
"Some of my university L2 students are under hypnosis and I ask them questions in their L2. As I know them, I am happy to see that they have no problem listening to one another, remembering what others said, that they are not afraid to speak when asked, telling stories they just imagined. For sure, those students can now perform better in their L2 than they usually can."

Palo Alto and Esalen Schools started to have an impact on L2 didactics not too long ago and their impact is not over yet.

However, it is interesting to point out that a new trend in psychology, transpersonal psychology and a new trend in communication studies, new communication, are having an impact on today's L2 didactics the way, a few decades ago, a new trend in psychology, behaviorist psychology and a new trend in linguistics, structural linguistics, had an impact on L2 didactics: the field of L2 didactics is constantly evolving.

Typical Teaching Procedures for a Radical Lesson

As this type of lesson is relatively new and also relies on the relation L2 teacher and learners succeed in creating, that relation varying from one teacher to another, the suggested procedures may not be suitable for everybody and therefore have to be adapted according to the L2 contexts, the students and the teachers.

1. The L2 teacher reads aloud a text chosen according to students' level and needs;

2. The L2 teacher reads the text aloud again, this time more slowly and with a baroque music background;
3. The L2 students close their eyes and the L2 teacher reads the text aloud again, this time faster and with a baroque music background;
4. L2 students use words and expressions they know with the help of games;
5. L2 students use their L2 in more complex contexts such as plays.

Beyond the Concept of L2 Didactics Paradigms

As already mentioned, paradigms are useful classifications of methods, techniques and approaches.

However, authors of different methods do not always specify to what paradigm they belong. In fact, many of them do not even know they belong to such and such a paradigm.

Paradigms are major trends in the way people think and develop according to the evolution of civilizations. For instance, the classical paradigm influenced and was influenced by great civilizations of the past while structuralism and behaviorism influenced many area of study such as linguistics, psychology, literature, anthropology and so on. Today, applications of cognitive psychology, constructivism, socioconstructivism and vicariant learning influence the fields of psychology and education in general. A paradigm could be seen as a reaction of the human thought to its global environment.

The use of a specific L2 paradigm cannot solve all the problems encountered in L2 teaching as the use of a specific L2 paradigm may not be suitable for a teacher, a student or even an institution, such as a school, a college or a university.

That is the reason why it is useful and even important for L2 teachers to be able to use approaches, methods and techniques from different paradigms because that way, they can adapt their teaching according to learners' needs and institutions' policies. In fact, it is widely acknowledged, even by their developers, that a paradigm or method cannot be exactly applied or followed in the classroom.

Indeed, as the following testimonies illustrate, sometimes, L2 teachers cannot apply the paradigm they believe in.

Testimony 19: My L2 Teacher Resigns Because He Believes in His Teaching Method

The following event happened in the Montréal area.

"Mr. Smith is a L2 professor at the junior college I attend.

Mr. Smith does not believe that a L2 can be taught the traditional way, using grammar and translation. He prefers a progressivist or behaviorist approach even though the college authorities believe in a classical approach.

Mr. Smith tells us what he wants to do and we agree with him.

He meets with the parents and tells them what he wants to do. They agree and decide to meet with the college authorities to let them know they would favor Mr. Smith's approach, a practical one, to the theoretical one in which the college authorities believe.

The college authorities explain to the parents that the approach they want to use has been used for hundreds of years and that therefore Mr. Smith cannot use another approach.

A few weeks later, Mr. Smith must resign from his position because the college authorities find him to be a trouble maker."

Testimony 20: I Make Compromises to Keep my Job as a L2 Teacher

The following event happened in the Montréal area.

"I teach English L2 for a high school and I do a lot of group oral repetitions because I use a behaviorist method.

The school principal tells me that other teachers find my courses too noisy and that my classes have to be quiet.

I then decide to give only written exercises although doing so goes against the principles of the method. My students are quiet and the principal is happy. I am not certain that my students learn much because I don't believe in the classical paradigm for L2 teaching.

I think of what happened to Mr. Smith and I would not like the same thing to happen to me. I therefore decide to use classical paradigm's techniques"

A paradigm also has to be chosen according to learners' goals and levels. L2 advanced learners wanting to improve their written skills could benefit from a classical paradigm course given by a college, while L2 beginners wishing to learn to speak could benefit from a progressivist paradigm course given by a language school.

It is therefore important to know that L2 courses do not always have the same goals and cannot answer the needs of every clientele. However, it could be problematic for learners who have to take a L2 course aiming at goals that differ from their own. It is therefore important that administrators, professors, teachers, learners and learners' parents (when appropriate) share the same goals and that the students be put in the right L2 level.

Table 2 summarizes goals and means of the L2 didactic paradigms.

Tab. 2: Aims of Eurocentric L2 Didactics Paradigms

Classical:
teaches *the written language*;
puts the emphasis on *the teacher or the professor*;
targets *the advanced learners*.

Progressivist:
teaches *the oral language*;
puts the emphasis on *the method*;
targets *beginners and intermediate learners*.

Behaviorist:
teaches *the oral language*;
puts the emphasis on *teaching*;
targets *beginners*.

Communicative:
teaches *the oral and the written language*;
puts the emphasis on *the use of the language and the learner*;
targets *intermediate learners*.

Radical:
teaches *the oral and the written language*;
puts the emphasis on *the use of the language and the learner as a person*;
targets *beginners, intermediate and advanced learners*

Questions to Explore the L2 Didactics Paradigms

Being more at ease in a L2 didactic paradigm or preferring one is not always a question of logic.

Indeed, many more or less conscious factors can influence the perception people have of a L2 didactic paradigm: a L2 teacher learners previously had, the area they specialized in, the way they learned a L2 and so on.

That is why, in order to help L2 teachers and administrators choose the right paradigm for their learners and themselves, a list of questions is provided below. The list, although not exhaustive, aims at giving clues to understand why learners and teachers could prefer a specific paradigm.

1. What is your L1?
2. Do you know how to write in your L1?
3. What L2 do you want to learn?
4. Why do you want to know the L2?
5. Do you speak one or many L2?
6. How did you learn your L2?
7. How did you learn to teach a L2?
8. What L2 methods or paradigms are you familiar with?
9. What is your best memory as a L2 learner?
10. Why?
11. Have you ever been shy or ashamed of speaking your L1?
12. If yes, why?
13. Have you ever been shy or ashamed of speaking your L2?
14. To which L2 methods or paradigms can you relate to?
15. Why?
16. Do you want to learn how to write or how to speak in the L2?
17. What level do you want to reach in the L2: beginner, intermediate or advanced?
18. Do you have difficulties reading or speaking in your L1?

Having described the L2 paradigms, it is now appropriate to choose one according to learners' needs.

As much as possible, the choice has to be made in accordance with the learners' education and culture. For example, an educated learner whose mother tongue and culture are Mandarin or Spanish will not learn the L2 the same way an illiterate learner whose mother tongue is an Aboriginal language. Indeed, Mandarin an Spanish are strong and dominant languages with a long writing tradition, while Aboriginal languages in general are not dominant languages and have none or almost no writing tradition.

Chapter 4:
A Suggested L2 Didactics Paradigm for Aboriginal Learners

In order to choose the most suitable way to teach a L2 to Aboriginal learners, traditional Aboriginal education must be described.

Elements of Aboriginal Teaching

> When the White thought of giving our children a White education, I think he must have known perfectly well that, in the future, he would create troubles for us, Indians. (Kapesh, 2019, p. 61)

Before looking at Aboriginal teaching per se, it is important to know what the word Aboriginal really means. In Canada, there are three groups of Aboriginal peoples (or First Peoples): the First Nations (or Indians, a term that many perceive as pejorative), the Inuit and the Métis. Those three groups are subject to different federal rules and regulations.

In Canada, many people of Aboriginal descent now live in communities created for them, but many people of Aboriginal descent now live elsewhere, mainly in large cities, such as Vancouver, Calgary, Winnipeg, Toronto or Montréal. In fact, it is not so easy to define exactly who is Aboriginal, because many Aboriginal peoples no longer speak their native language and no longer practice their traditional ways of living. Allain and Demers (2016, p. 6) say:

> Indeed, we must realise that the word Aboriginal can lead to confusion ... The word Aboriginal referring ... to the first inhabitants of a region, a country.

It is therefore important to remember that Aboriginal peoples may be very different from one another and, in fact, sometimes, it is almost impossible to know who is Aboriginal and who is not. This is the reason why Gatti (2009, p. 34), speaking of Aboriginal writers, says that:

> If it is true that identity comes from the subjective conscience that a person feels that distinguish her or him from the others ... And that identity is a project in constant movement, I propose a first general definition ...: an Aboriginal author is someone who considers and defines herself or himself as such.

The definition of who is an Aboriginal writer proposed by Gatti is important in an educational context, whereas an Aboriginal learner could also consider himself or herself as such. What will be said about Aboriginal education is nevertheless important for many Aboriginal learners, but not necessarily for every one of them.

Looking at Aboriginal teaching is, in a way, looking back at Paleolithic teaching. Indeed, as Paleolithic refers to a long period of time before the invention of writing, a fundamental trait of traditional Aboriginal teaching is the exclusive use of oral language.

As there is no written document from that period, the only way for us to see how teaching was done in those ancient times is probably to look at how teaching is done presently in Paleolithic cultures of today or, in the Canadian context, to look at Elders from Aboriginal communities who remember how teaching was done not too long ago.

Speaking about the Inuit ways of learning, the anthropologist Saladin d'Anglure (2006, p. 34) says that ' ... in such a society, knowledge was acquired by imitation, sensory experience or oral transmission; by dreams also or contact with the spirits'. In fact, in some Aboriginal cultures, the Elders are the oral traditions' transmitters and the Shamans are the dreams' interpreters.

The late Matthew Iserhoff, a Cree Elder from Mistissini and a highly respected educator, once told the author that traditional teaching is based on the three Ls methodology: Look, Listen and Learn. These three words are, in fact, at the heart of traditional teaching. It happens in a meaningful context, involves many physical senses and produces immediate results. Researchers in the field of traditional Aboriginal education elaborate on the three Ls methodology. For example, according to Toulouse (2011, p. 1),

> In traditional (time immemorial to colonial period) education practices of Aboriginal children and youth were, historically, a community responsibility...

Elements of Aboriginal Teaching

Each of the 50 Nations in Canada had its own unique way of ensuring its young were culturally and linguistically educated. Elders and key cultural teachers worked with children in an engaging manner through observation, hands-on activities, reflection, storytelling, and practice ... Education was defined as a lifelong process that honoured and valued the learner.

Researchers in the field of traditional Aboriginal education also mention diverse characteristics of traditional Aboriginal education and teaching techniques.

For example, Gélinas (2013, p. 178) mentions 20 traditional techniques:

The community is of the highest importance;
The tradition is oral;
Present time dominates;
The world is seen through myths;
Goals are reached with patience;
Property is often communitarian;
Presents are considered as elements of social cohesion;
Work is often motivated by the needs of the group;
Getting older is seen as a source of wisdom;
Direct visual contact is perceived as of aggressive nature;
Silences are respected and do not lead to a lack of comfort;
Self-confidence is not a communitarian element;
Listening capacity is put forward;
To speak softly is normal;
To nod means to understand;
Handshake is light, unthreatening;
Collective decisions are made out of consensus;
To believe in the harmony of nature is put forward;
The family is the extended family;
People react to group praise.

Other researchers point out less characteristics. For example, according to Ignace (2016, p. vii) First peoples learning has nine characteristics:

- 'Learning ultimately supports the well-being of the self, the family, the community, the land, the spirits, and the ancestors.

- Learning is holistic, reflexive, reflective, experiential, and relational (focused on connectedness, on reciprocal relationships, and a sense of place).
- Learning involves recognizing the consequences of one's actions.
- Learning involves generational roles and responsibilities.
- Learning recognizes the role of indigenous knowledge.
- Learning is embedded in memory, history, and story.
- Learning involves patience and time.
- Learning requires exploration of one's identity.
- Learning involves recognizing that some knowledge is sacred and only shared with permission and/or in certain situations.'

With regard to L2 didactics per se, Allain, Demers, Grigoroiu and Pelletier (2017, p. 10) call attention to seven characteristics of traditional Aboriginal teaching:

1. 'The transactional distance, the relation between the teacher and the learners and also among the learners themselves, must favor communication in order for learning to happen. It is not possible, in such a context, for the teacher to use an authoritative approach. The creation of this transactional distance that favors communication requires from the teacher a great deal of confidence, humility, patience and attentive listening to learners;

2. The oral language is put forward. As a matter of fact, for Aboriginals, traditions, culture, history, all knowledge, in fact, is transmitted orally;

3. Learning is always practical;

4. Work is done in groups and in a collaborative way;

5. Learning is holistic;

6. Communication is done from person to person and takes into account all the person's dimensions: the physical, emotional, intellectual and spiritual dimensions (i.e. the dimensions of internal world, of dream, of imagination, of altered states of consciousness);

7. The evaluation has no importance in itself because it is made on a spontaneous and continuous way.'

The first characteristic mentioned above, the importance of the creation of a trustful transactional distance, a strong pedagogical relationship, is also emphasized by Battiste (2002), Chartrand (2010) and Toulouse (2015) among others. This is not surprising since, as already mentioned, in the context of Aboriginal cultures, human beings have four important facets: physical, emotional, intellectual and spiritual. The traditional teachers, the oral tradition transmitters, the Elders[31] and the Shamans, know the importance of this strong pedagogical relationship. If the Elders have this strong pedagogical relationship because they have the respect of their communities, the Shamans[32] go even further to intensify it by the use of diverse techniques (drums, dance, etc.) in order to induce an altered state of consciousness that will improve the learning experience.

An altered state of consciousness is defined by Clothes and Lewis-Williams (2001, p. 14) as: 'States of consciousness are linked ... However, we may consider that they are parts of a continuous set (a continuum). At one end of this set there is what we can call the awake consciousness. At the other end, there is the deep trance'. That way, the Shaman will be able to better help the community when it is needed (for ceremonies, medical purposes, etc.) as mentioned by Demers and Simard (2015).

Moreover, the cultural genocide that happened to Aboriginal peoples in Canada for more than a century renders this trustful pedagogical relationship even more important. It is difficult to trust anyone related to eurocentric teaching after such a long period of mistrust. The cultural genocide created many problems in Aboriginal communities in Canada, one of them being poor self-esteem. On that aspect, Toulouse (no date, p. 2) says that:

> A growing body of research demonstrates that Aboriginal students' self-esteem is a key factor in their school success ... An educational environment that honours the culture, language and worldview of the Aboriginal student is critical to this process. The curriculum and pedagogy of schools need to meaningfully represent and include Aboriginal people's contributions, innovations and inventions. Aboriginal students require schools in all aspects to honour 'who they are' and 'where they have come from'. Aboriginal self-esteem is described as the balanced and positive interconnection between the physical, emotional/mental, intellectual and spiritual realms.

It is important here to underline the deculturation process intended by authorities of the residential schools who adhered to this federal government endeavor. The deculturation process aims at the disappearance

---

[31] Elders are very important for Aboriginal Peoples because they know and preserve the language, the culture and the traditions that are in danger of extinction. For oral societies, they are the links between the past and the present.
[32] See Walsh (2011) for further details on shamanism.

of a culture and a language. It leads to a cultural genocide or, even worst, a genocide. According to the *Commission de vérité et réconciliation du Canada* (2012, p. 1), Hector Langevin, Minister of Public Works of Canada, said, in 1883, the following about this cultural genocide:

> To educate the children correctly, we must separate them from their family. Some people may think it is a drastic measure, but we have no other choice if we wish to civilize them.

Indeed, from 1879 to 1996 (dates contested by some), the federal government of Canada took away Aboriginal children from their families and put them in religious residential schools to educate them. However, history shows that many children were abused and some even died in those residential schools. According to the *National Inquiry into Missing and Murdered Indigenous Women and Girls* (2019, p. 23)

> The history of colonization has altered Inuit, First Nations, and Métis Peoples' relationships to their culture and identity through targeted policies designed to sever their cultural and kin connections ... Cultural rights are inseparable from human rights, and within the international rights context, are defined as the right of access to, participation in, and enjoyment of culture.

It is therefore not surprising that, after such a genocide, many researchers in the field of Aboriginal education underline the importance of going back to traditional Aboriginal cultures. For example, Maina (1999) emphasizes the importance of reaffirming the validity of Aboriginal cultures. This is also the reason why Campeau (2016) underlines the importance of a place-based curriculum and instruction: eurocentric schools reflect the cultural values of the dominant society and are, therefore, not adapted to Aboriginal learners. Grigoroiu (2016), recognizing the importance of oral narratives in traditional Aboriginal teaching, discusses the use of legends and storytelling in teaching reading and developing oral expression, noting that oral narratives are still in use in modern societies. On the same topic, Rahan (2009, p. 25) states that:

> The influence of culture on the academic performance of Aboriginal students has been studied for decades. Many educators and researchers attribute the low success rates and frequent alienation of Aboriginal students to the cultural clash they experience in a school environment which contradicts their traditional values and norms.

Yunkaporta (2009) identifies eight ways to help teachers improve their teaching practices with Aboriginal learners, while Osborne (1996) identifies nine strategies aiming at the same purpose. On the same subject of improving teaching strategies, Gower and Bryne (2012, p. 386) say that 'to embrace differences in knowledge, experiences and understanding' are important characteristics of culturally competent teachers'.

Of all the elements of traditional Aboriginal education given by researchers, some seem more important than others because they keep coming up in the research literature. They are:

1. Exclusive use of oral language;
2. A trustful relationship between the teacher and the learners;
3. A strong self-esteem;
4. The use of many senses in the learning/teaching process (looking, listening, feeling …);
5. Learning is a group process;
6. A learner is a person and has four facets: physical, intellectual, emotional and spiritual;
7. The teacher has to be aware of the Aboriginal learners' needs;
8. Elements of Aboriginal cultures have to be integrated in the curriculum (traditional legends, ceremonies, feasts, etc.).

The Wheels

Moreover, as the wheel is often mentioned in the review of literature in Aboriginal studies, it is possible to create a traditional Aboriginal education wheel with the eight elements listed above. The wheel symbolizes the cyclical conception of the world in Aboriginal cultures and world view.

It is also useful to know that colors are often used in Aboriginal cultures. Although their meanings may vary according to a specific culture, generally, the red color is related to the spiritual facet of human beings, the yellow color to their emotional facet, the black color to their physical facet and the white color to their intellectual facet, as in the following example. Figure 3 represents a traditional Aboriginal education wheel:

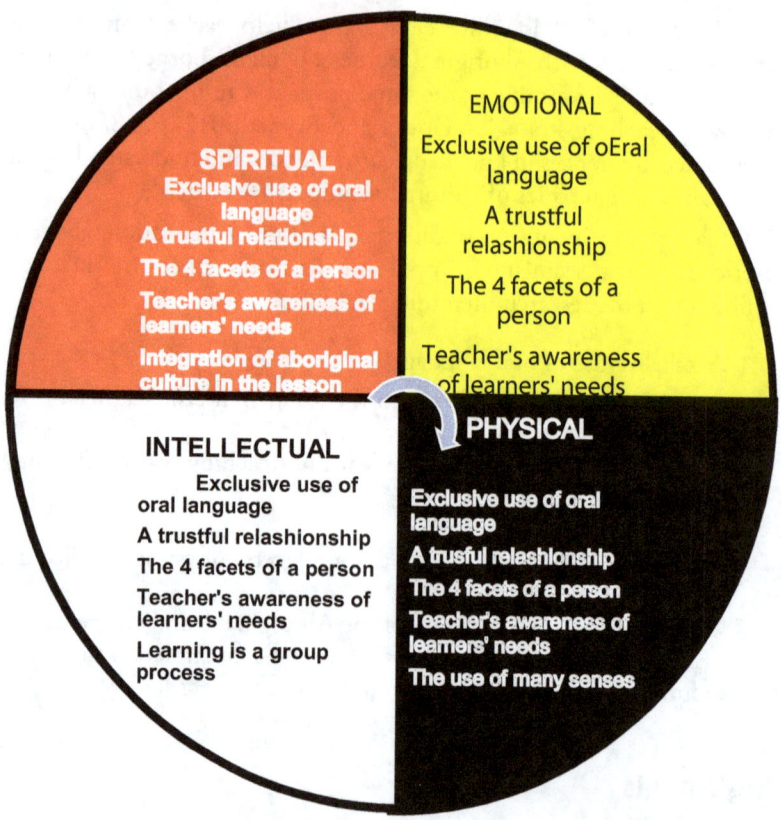

Fig. 3: A Traditional Aboriginal Education Wheel

Wheels are used to represent many aspects of Aboriginal cultures. Medicine wheels are particularly popular in Aboriginal cultures and Joseph (2013, p. 1) explains the use of the medicine wheel in Aboriginal cultures the following way:

> ... medicine wheels represent the alignment and continuous interaction of the physical, emotional, mental, and spiritual realities. The circle shape represents the interconnectivity of all aspects of one's being, including the connection with natural world. Medicine wheels are frequently believed to be the circle of awareness of the individual self; the circle of knowledge that provides the power we each have over our own lives.

The Circles

Circles are important in Aboriginal cultures, especially the talking circles. When a group of people get together to solve a problem or to speak about a particular topic concerning the community, they create a talking circle. In a talking circle, an essential norm is to listen attentively to the participant who speaks, so that the wisdom of the speaker's words may be heard. Indeed, according to Graveline (1996. p. 178) 'through respectful listening we are better able to enter into another's experience through their words'. Talking circles must follow certain rules and, for example, Tufts (1998, p. 12) states the following rules of a talking circle:

One person speaks at a time.
No one is forced to speak.
No time limit is placed on what the speaker has to say.
Everyone in the circle listens respectfully to the words of the speaker.
The person on the speaker's left is the next one to speak.
No one is permitted to criticize or speak negatively of what is shared in the circle.

Moreover, according to the web site of First Nations' Pedagogy online (n.d., p. 1) on talking circles,

Several varied objects are used by different First Nations peoples to facilitate the talking circle. Some peoples use a talking stick, others a talking feather, while still others use a peace pipe, a sacred shell, a wampum belt, or other selected object. The main point of using the sacred object, is that whoever is holding the object in their hand has the right to speak. The circle itself is considered sacred.

In addition, Aboriginal groups have values that are specific to their community. For example, Saulis (2019), a Maliseet Elder and scholar, identifies seven values for two First Nations:

1. The Ojibwa Seven Grandfather Teachings are: love, respect, bravery, honesty, humility, truth and wisdom;
2. the Micmac Seven Sacred Gifts of Life are: love, honesty, humility, respect, truth, patience and wisdom.

Suggestions for L2 Teaching to Aboriginal Peoples

As already mentioned, L2 teaching is also an art and many L2 teachers already experienced teaching to Aboriginal learners without any particular training in the field and some of them had very successful experiences, because they instinctively adapted their teaching to their Aboriginal learners. Here is an example of such an experience.

A Successful Experience of L2 Teaching to Cree Learners

Many experienced L2 teachers are surprised to see that techniques that seem to work well with their learners in general do not necessarily work well with their Aboriginal learners. This is because they are not aware of the specificity of Aboriginal teaching. Pelletier in Allain, Demers, Pelletier (2013) provides a good example of that. This is a summary of Pelletier's first teaching experience with Aboriginal learners.

Pelletier was teaching English L2 to Cree adult learners. Although she had a thorough knowledge of andragogy, she was surprised by what she observed in her learners.

First, she realized that she had to respect the silence of her learners. Later on in her career, she had the chance to work with Cree colleagues and understood that silence was pleasant and she did not have to speak with her colleagues as much as she would have to in a eurocentric environment. She nevertheless succeeded in creating a trustful relationship with her learners and with her colleagues and was much appreciated by both.

Then, she realized that her learners did not seem to work well on their own, but were working well in groups. In eurocentric education, working on your own is valorized, but not in Aboriginal education.

Pelletier also realized that she had to listen to her learners in spite of their silence. Observation can tell many things that are not verbally expressed. By observing her learners, she noticed that they very much liked to work with computers and that there were not enough computers in the classroom. Fortunately, she was able to get more computers for her learners.

Pelletier finally realized that she was using a very eurocentric method that did not matched her learners' culture. She therefore integrated Cree culture elements in her teaching. For example, one of her learners had a presentation to make in front of the class, a task really difficult for someone who is not used to make a presentation in front of a group. In order to alleviate the stress, she decided to use a circular table in the classroom for the students who came to listen to the presentation. Everyone was then sitting in a circle, something familiar to their way of communicating. They came to the presentation out of respect for the presenter, respect being an important Cree value (even if Pelletier did not know that at the time).

All the learners came to the presentation and learners from other groups also came to show their solidarity with the presenter.

Although this is only an example, it gives a good idea of the differences between eurocentric education and Aboriginal education.

Indeed, the traditional Aboriginal education wheel shows Aboriginal students' needs as follows:

1. exclusive use of oral language;
2. a trustful relationship;
3. the four facets of a person;
4. teacher's awareness of learners' needs;
5. a strong self-esteem;
6. the use of many senses;
7. learning is a group process;
8. integration of Aboriginal culture in the lesson.

In order to help L2 teachers, suggestions are proposed below to answer the specific needs of their Aboriginal learners.

Exclusive Use of Oral Language

As shown above, L2 didactics contains many paradigms. Of all the paradigms, only the communicative and the radical paradigms focus on oral communication.

A Trustful Relationship

Aboriginal students also need a trustful relationship between the teacher and the learners. A way to attain this trustful relationship between the teacher and learners is for the teacher and the learners to meet as a group before the beginning of the L2 course. The meeting, that can be seen as a part of lesson zero, as it will be seen later in the text, is carried in the learners' L1 in the presence of an interpreter (or, whenever possible, by an Elder who can act as an interpreter) if the teacher does not know the learners' L1. During the meeting, the teacher asks the learners the reasons why they want to learn the L2, their expectations and their fears. The teacher also explains the way the method works and what could be expected from the learners. The teacher and the learners define their roles in the learning process and what linguistic outcomes are to be expected from the learners. At the end of the meeting, the teacher and the learners as a group agree on what is to be done by the group, including the teacher. It is not recommended, however, for the learners to sign a document out of respect for Aboriginal cultures, because writing is not a part of these cultures.

Moreover, for all the L2 lessons, it is important for the L2 teacher to greet the learners when they arrive to the class.

The Four Facets of a Person[33]

Aboriginal learners have to be considered as persons with emotional, physical, intellectual and spiritual needs. This will happen when L2 teachers see themselves as guides or transmitters, not as traditional eurocentric teachers who possess the knowledge and who need to stick to a method or a program without regards for their learners.

Teacher's Awareness of Learners' Needs

Aboriginal learners also need L2 teachers to be aware of their needs. It does not suffice for L2 teachers to know the L2 language and the eurocentric teaching techniques that focus on good performances at quizzes and tests.

---

[33] Lemaire (2021) uses role-playing games with future teachers because, according to her, those games imply the four facets of a person and therefore favor the reconciliation of Aboriginal and non-Aboriginal groups in Canada.

A Strong Self-Esteem

The Aboriginal learner also needs a strong self-esteem. As a matter of fact, self-esteem is a key factor in L2 teaching and has been underlined by many researchers in the field of L2 didactics. For example, Yang (2012, p. 1) states that:

> Learners who possess high self-esteem and positive personal image have more chances to succeed in learning. The reason for this phenomenon is that those people usually dare to adventure and are not afraid of making mistakes which give them more opportunities to communicate in a foreign language. On the contrary, people with low self-esteem lose many chances under the same circumstances.

In order to improve learner's self-esteem, L2 teachers can show learners openness, careful, patient listening, and encouragement. This will happen when the L2 teacher considers his or her learners as persons and as equals and shows respect for their cultures.

The Use of Many Senses

Aboriginal learners have to use many senses: they have to see, to listen and to feel what the L2 teacher is transmitting. In order to do that, the L2 teacher can use a blackboard with chalks of different colors, posters, gestures, songs, music, computers, various technologies and the Internet.

Learning Is a Group Process

Aboriginal learners learn better in a group where they can share the knowledge transmitted by the L2 teacher. In order to do that, learners should be sitting in a circle; the L2 teacher should be able to sit in the circle, because he or she is the learners' equal, but should also be able to stand inside and out of the circle to help learners share among themselves the knowledge transmitted by the teacher.

Integration of Aboriginal Culture in the Class

L2 teachers have to integrate elements of Aboriginal culture in the class (and the program). This can be achieved by:

1. having Aboriginal paintings, posters and decorations in the classroom;
2. using the L2 to speak of elements of traditional Aboriginal cultures (such as hunting, fishing, berry picking, walking out and other ceremonies, etc.);
3. sharing traditional food;
4. listening in the L2 to traditional legends;
5. watching in the L2 movies and documentaries with Aboriginal content;
6. reading in the L2 texts with Aboriginal content or Aboriginal authors' writings;
7. inviting Elders to address the class in the L2;
8. having Aboriginal guests to address the class in the L2;
9. listening to soft music (baroque, classical, Aboriginal, etc.) while the learners read and write in the L2;
10. asking the learners to imagine a dream induced in the L2 by the teacher.

As Aboriginal education's goal is learners' empowerment, the radical paradigm is the best suited paradigm to successfully teach L2 to Aboriginal learners, because the radical paradigm aims at learners' empowerment.

Indeed, according to Saulis, a Maliseet scholar and Elder (2019, p. 12):

> Empowerment is a holistic experience, in that it affects our mental (the way we think), spirit (the way we acquire and sense meaning in life), emotional (the way we feel about ourselves and the world), and the physical (the actions we take).

From the description of the traditional Aboriginal education, it is clear that the L2 paradigm that is best suited for Aboriginal learners is the radical paradigm for many reasons. Indeed, in that paradigm, learners are seen as whole persons with their four facets and the teacher is seen as a guide, a transmitter. Moreover, in that paradigm, oral language is of the outmost importance and the learners are treated with respect and so is their culture.

In our opinion and as already mentioned, the radical paradigm is in fact the best paradigm for any teacher wanting to teach the oral L2 and any learner, Aboriginal or not, who wants to master it.

Integration of elements of the learner's culture in the L2 class, program and the curriculum is however more specific to Aboriginal learners.

As a matter of fact, L2 teachers, education consultants and researchers from diverse Aboriginal education organizations such as the Kativik School Board for the Inuit learners, the Cree School Board for the Cree learners, the *Institut Tsahkapesh* for the Innu learners and the *Kahnawà:ke* Education Center for the Mohawk learners are already integrating elements of Aboriginal cultures in their L2 curricula. For example, the Cree School Board made an English L2 learning situation focusing on the walking out ceremony, a typical Aboriginal tradition for young children who go outside of the traditional tipi for the first time.

Moreover, the curricula for Aboriginal learners of many Canadian Ministries of Education also use elements of different Aboriginal cultures to teach English L2 and other school subjects. For example, in March 2021, the Ontario Ministry of Education (*Indigenous Education Strategy*, p. 1) site says:

> Ontario's Indigenous Education Strategy is supporting First Nation, Métis and Inuit students to achieve their full potential ... This strategy has been designed to improve opportunities for First Nation, Métis and Inuit students, to increase the knowledge and awareness of all students about Indigenous histories, cultures and perspectives and contributions.

Furthermore, even the federal Department of Employment and Social Development Canada has been working in collaboration with *the Université du Québec à Chicoutimi* on a curriculum that integrates elements of Aboriginal cultures (mainly Innu) to offer French L2 courses to Aboriginal federal civil servants who want to learn French L2.

The integration of the L1 cultures (or C1) elements in the L2 class, program or curriculum is in fact a characteristic of L2 programs to Aboriginal learners.

Part II:

Practical Considerations

In this part, different procedures used in L2 teaching will be explored.

The procedures are grouped in three categories: those used before teaching, those used as tools in the teaching process and those used after teaching. Some procedures can be used in more than one category: lesson zero suggested procedures have to be used before teaching and also in the teaching process, when needed, while error correction techniques have to be used after teaching and also in the teaching process, when necessary.

As mentioned earlier, the suggested procedures have to be adapted according to students' needs, age, L1 and other factors and also to teachers' personality and different educational contexts. However, they have all been successfully used. When necessary, specific elements are pointed out to help L2 teachers to Aboriginal learners better answer their learners' needs.

It is in the practice that one fully realizes that L2 teaching is often more an art than a science and so is teaching in general, for that matter.

Chapter 5:
Before Teaching Procedures

Class Preparation

Class preparation takes into account the content the teacher intends to teach, the learning objects, the procedures, and the techniques to be used.

All the elements suggested here can be used for class preparation, a crucial step in L2 lessons.

However, although it is essential to have a good class preparation, it is also very useful to have an alternative class preparation just in case the class preparation one intended to use does not work for whatever reason. As a matter of fact, one has to be aware that one constantly has to adapt the preparation to one's learners. That way, learners do not have to constantly adapt to class preparation. Indeed, it is important to remember that, at least in the radical paradigm, L2 teachers must listen to their learners.

Listening to learners is even more crucial with Aboriginal learners.

The L2 Program

It is very difficult to design a useful class preparation without a L2 program.

In a L2 program, as in any other educational program, there are terminal objectives learners have to reach at the end of the program and intermediate objectives learners have to reach at specific times in the program in order to for them to reach the terminal objectives.

Usually, the program is given to the teachers by the institution where they work, but it is not always the case. If there is no program, the L2 teacher will have to determine the terminal and intermediate objectives of the course in consultation with the institution authorities.

It is important to know. as soon as possible, the learners' level or levels at the beginning of the program and the level or levels they should be at the end of the program. When the terminal objectives are impossible to reach for a majority of learners, the terminal objectives should be adapted to learners' level.

The objectives of the program are usually divided according to language skills in the broad sense.

There are four traditional language skills: listening, speaking, reading and writing. In the radical paradigm, there are more four more categories of language skills: grammar skills, interaction skills, strategic skills and cultural skills. Although there are no consensus among the authors on specific definitions of those skills, they can be broadly defined as follows: grammar skills comprise pronunciation, syntactic and lexical skills, interaction skills refer to the way a message can be effectively communicated, strategic skills allow speakers to start and keep on speaking and cultural skills refer to adequate use of L2 gestures, levels and registers.

It is crucial to know what level learners have to reach in every skill.

Needless to say that, with Aboriginal learners, the L2 program must include elements of Aboriginal cultures.

The Technology

L2 teaching (and even teaching in general) has always been linked to technology in the various stages of their evolution from the prehistoric days to the invention of writing, of printing, of audio-visual and of computer or multimedia technologies.

L2 didacticians do not have a specific knowledge of language teaching during the prehistoric ages except for the fact that, in that era, many people had to learn a L2 in order to exchange goods. It is even likely that, in those days, human beings used to speak more languages than they do today: as a matter of fact, as already mentioned, Australian Indigenous people were already multilingual when European explorers first came to that land and it is probable that the same situation was not different in other parts of the prehistoric world. For teaching in general though, it is known that, in those days, there were masters and disciples, because

Elders and Shamans were providing their teaching orally and legends were transmitted orally from generations to generations. Even after the invention of writing, great masters such as Buddha, Socrates and Jesus never wrote anything.

With the invention of writing, a phenomenon that happened at least five thousand years ago, L2 teaching as well as teaching in general dramatically changed because, for the first time, people could and even had to learn how to read and write.

The invention of printing in the fifteenth century of the common era allowed a democratization of reading and, that way, of L2 teaching.

In the middle of the twentieth century, the use of audio-visual technologies allowed learning and teaching or the oral language without the need of a native speaker while before that, in the progressivist paradigm for instance, the oral language was taught by a teacher who had a L1 knowledge of the L2.

More recently, the use of computers and Internet has allowed L2 teachers and students to access a great number of written, visual, and oral documents of all kinds, that way deeply transforming L2 teaching and facilitating L2 learning.

The use of computers and Internet is essential to Aboriginal leaners because it requires the use of many senses, looking, listening and touching.

Learning Objects[34]

Although still new in the field of L2 teaching, the concept of learning objects is widely used in other areas of education, in distance education for example: it refers to all the objects used in teaching and learning and is closely linked to technologies.

For a long time, manuscripts were the preferred learning objects, but have gradually been replaced by books. However, with the use of multimedia technologies, the diversity of learning objects is constantly growing.

---

[34] Of course, the use of traditional Aboriginal objects such as drums and talking sticks should be encouraged.

L2 teachers should now be able to use a panoply of learning objects allowing them to adapt their teaching according to various learners' levels, learning styles and interests and, of course, to their own personal preferences.

When needed, however, L2 teachers should be able to collect and create their own learning objects.

With Aboriginal learners, learning objects should be traditional Aboriginal objects, whenever possible, and the colors of the objects should be, whenever possible, traditional Aboriginal colors like black, yellow, white and red.

Classroom Layout

Classroom layout is a characteristic of the L2 paradigm used.

In the classical, progressivist and behaviorist paradigms, the learners' chairs face the teacher's desk. In the communicative paradigm, the learners sit in small groups or in a horseshoe way and the teacher sits in front of the learners. In the radical paradigm, the learners sit in circles and the teacher can go from one circle to another.

With Aboriginal learners, as mentioned before, the teacher sits in a circle with the learners as in the radical paradigm.

Preparation to Class

Preparation to class depends on the way the teacher intends to tackle his or her class in accordance with the L2 paradigm used.

In the communicative and radical paradigms for example, the transactional distance, the rapport the teacher wishes to create with the learners to favor the communication of messages, is the main goal of the L2 course.

Transactional Distance

The concept of transactional distance is commonly used in the area of distance education because many people are under the impression that the physical distance, an intrinsic component of distance education, creates a distance in the relation between the teacher and the students, even though it is not always the case.

Transactional distance firstly refers to the distance involved in an information exchange between two individuals. That distance has, in fact, less to do with the actual physical distance. Indeed, most people have sadly been in the presence of teachers or professors who would purposely create a distance between them and the student, to make sure students would stay away from them.

Transactional distance also refers to the distance there is between the content of a learning object and the learners: indeed, in a face to face context where teachers and learners share the same space, that distance should be insignificant because the teacher explains to learners what they do not understand about the content of the learning objects.

Martindale, on the *Athabasca University Resource Site* (2002, p. 5) defines transactional distance as follows:

> Transactional distance is positively related to the size of the learning group, familiarity of language and dialects, the qualities of the medium through which the signal is transmitted. These include issues of noise, speed, and lag. This theory includes internal didactic conversations as proposed by Holmberg. In this case the learning material becomes the stimulus for dialogue that occurs within the learner and this produces learning... A textbook and study guide with only internal dialogue would be considered to have a high transactional distance. A synchronous discussion done through audio conferencing would be lower.

Transactional distance is an important component in teaching in general but in L2 teaching to Aboriginal learners, it is absolutely crucial.

Indeed, in order to create a context favorable to L2 teaching and learning, Aboriginal learners must be able to trust their teacher in a way that allows them not to be afraid of speaking or making mistakes. That will happen only if the relation created between the Aboriginal learners and their teacher and, ideally among the Aboriginal learners themselves, allows it or if, in other words, the transactional distance allows it.

Indeed, at least in the radical paradigm, language teaching favors an optimal exchange between all participants (teacher and learners).

Building an adequate transactional distance is not an easy thing to do: one has to create trust without familiarity, get close without being too close.

A way to do that is to create a pedagogical relationship[35] with every learner: every learner has to know that his or her learning is important to the teacher who is there to help him or her learn. When everybody feels at ease, many problems, including class management problems, are solved.

With Aboriginal learners, as already mentioned, the creation of a good transactional distance is key to successful L2 teaching.

Preparation to class also involves being psychologically ready and well rested because L2 teachers can be seen as actors or musicians. Indeed, as in performing arts, L2 teaching necessitates a lot of energy and flexibility, sustained attention and an excellent knowledge of procedures and techniques that will be described in the next chapter.

With Aboriginal learners, it is also important to be aware of traditional Aboriginal cultures. Whenever possible, it is also important for teachers to be present in the classroom before the learners arrive in order to welcome them.

---

[35] To create a pedagogical relationship, Gauthier and Jeffrey (1999) suggest using seduction in a broad sense.

Chapter 6:
Teaching Procedures

Teaching the Oral Components of the Language

For many L2 teachers, teaching oral skills is a challenge because learners can then be more undisciplined and noisier than when writing skills are taught. However, as oral skills are more important for most learners than written skills, they have to be taught. Moreover, for Aboriginal learners, oral skills are of the outmost importance, since traditional Aboriginal teaching is oral.

Teaching Listening Skills

Listening is the most important of the four traditional language skills (oral comprehension, oral expression, written comprehension and written expression) for a majority of learners and is also absolutely indispensable for language acquisition. It is also the language skill human beings use the most.

Many authors such as Demers (1992) and Krashen (1985) emphasized the crucial importance of comprehension in L2 acquisition, which requires a lot of listening for the oral language and a lot of reading for the written language.

Krashen (1981, 1982) also proposes two hypotheses, two theoretical models that enhance comprehension: the affective filter and the comprehensible input or intake model.

To understand those models, a distinction between L2 acquisition and L2 learning has to be made: L2 acquisition is an unconscious process that leads to the mastery of a language, while learning is a conscious process that leads to the knowledge of the grammar rules of a language.

L2 acquisition requires comprehension and is more important than L2 learning for most people.

That distinction between acquisition and learning (seen by Krashen as a dichotomy) raised a huge controversy in the area of L2 teaching and learning at the time. It is nevertheless a good way to understand the importance of comprehension in the field of L2 didactics.

According to the affective filter model, certain affective factors play a very important role in L2 acquisition: learners need a good self-image, have to be motivated and the class atmosphere has to be relaxed.

According to the comprehensible input model, L2 learners have to be exposed to linguistic data that are neither too easy nor too difficult for them: linguistic data difficulty level has to be just a little higher than that of the learners in order for intake to take place. Krashen uses the equation *intake = i + I* (where *i* stands for input and *I* stands form new linguistic material) to summarize his model.[36]

Few L2 didacticians would deny today the importance of oral comprehension because of the growing quantity and variety of oral texts most people are exposed to.

There is, indeed, a great quantity and variety of oral texts: songs, poems, plays, news, interviews, informal conversations and so on. There are, of course, numerous factors having an impact on listening such as the speaker's pronunciation, speech flow and tone, the listener's linguistic and background knowledge, attention level and interests, the background noise level etc.

Because of the variety of oral texts and the multiplicity of factors involved in oral comprehension, there are many techniques that can be used to help learners practice and enhance their listening skills. Those skills can be grouped in two categories, intensive listening and extensive listening.

Extensive listening is listening for content. There are two types of extensive listening exercises, skimming and scanning: in skimming exercises, learners are asked to grasp the general meaning of an oral text and in scanning exercises, learners are asked to find specific bits of information of an oral text.

---

[36] Kraschen's comprehensible input model is in line with Vygotsky's (1978) zone of proximal development concept.

Intensive listening is the practice of listening skills per se.

There exists a large variety of exercises and texts, however, because of the general nature of the present book, only one exercise and one type of text will be described.

As an example of a listening skill exercise, an intensive listening exercise will be proposed and the selected text will be a song because of the popularity of that specific listening skill exercise, especially with Aboriginal learners.

Since traditional Aboriginal teaching is based on the Look, Listen and Learn principle and because the teaching is provided by an Elder, Aboriginal learners have very good listening skills. Indeed, listening is a part of most Aboriginal cultures.

The procedure can be as follows:

1. Using the L2, the teacher gives the name of the singer, the composer and details about the type of song, etc.;
2. Learners listen to the song twice;
3. The teacher gives learners a written version of the song in which words are missing;
4. Learners listen to the song again, this time filling in the blanks;
5. The teacher gives listeners the missing words;
6. The teacher explains the words and expressions learners do not understand;
7. Learners listen to the song once more: this time though, the teacher and learners sing the song with the singer;
8. The teacher sings the song with the learners.

Teaching Speaking Skills

The teaching of speaking requires time and patience from the teacher and courage from learners.

It is important however, not to force learners to speak because it may discourage or intimidate them although they must be encouraged to speak as often as possible.

Although teachers cannot force learners to speak, some learners who speak too much have to be stopped in a gentle way to give more time for other learners to speak: learners who speak too much can otherwise create tensions in the group, sometimes resulting in class management problems. With Aboriginal learners, however, it is not too often that some learners will speak too much, because speaking is not an important component in most Aboriginal cultures.

There are many procedures the L2 teacher can use to teach speaking: those procedures can be classified in three categories according to the students' levels (beginners, intermediate and advanced learners). For example:

1. Beginners can be asked to describe the classroom, their home or a picture;
2. Intermediate learners can be asked to speak about their next or latest vacations or their hobbies;
3. Advanced learners can be asked to give their opinion about a topic or to do a presentation.

Aboriginal learners do not speak easily and their silence should be respected as much as possible.

Teaching Interaction Skills

Interaction implies listening and speaking. Interaction can be defined as the capacity to verbally react to a question or an argument from the teacher or another learner.

Interaction skills can be practiced in many ways: brainstorming, discussing and debating imply interaction skills.

However, as Aboriginal learners interact better as a group, a good way to practice interaction with them is to give them a group project.

For example, a good way to teach interaction skills could be as follows.

1- The teacher proposes a few projects;
2- The learners discuss the projects and chose one;
3- The learners work together on the project and realize it. The project could be the organization of a visit, the decoration of the classroom and, for Aboriginal learners, it could be the invitation of an Elder to address the class.

An Induced Daydream: The Forest[37]

Another good procedure to teach the oral skills is an induced daydream. It works well with Aboriginal learners, is inspired by the radical paradigm (more specifically by Jung's analytical psychology) and addresses the spiritual aspect of the person: here is an example.

The following exercise can be used with intermediate and advanced learners.

Before starting the induced dream, the teacher can write of the board a few words and explain them to help his or her learners understand better what the teacher says in the dream.

For the following dream, the words written on the board could be: forest, path, key, house, brook and wall.

The learners sit in a circle while the teacher stands out of the circle and says the following:

We will now do an induced daydream. Please sit comfortably, close your eyes and try to visualize the dream I tell you.

There is a forest in front of you. How is the forest? Is it big or is it small? Is it cold or warm? Is it a tropical forest or not? How do you feel? Are you comfortable or not? Are you cold or warm? Get closer to the forest and look at the trees: are they small or big? What season is it: winter, spring, summer or fall? Do you see leaves, animals, birds? What do you see? Are you on your own or with a friend or family member? How do you feel? In the forest, you see a path: is it large or narrow? Take the path and walk through the forest. How do you feel? Keep on walking and suddenly, you see a key on the ground. How is the key? Is it big or small? Is it an old key or a new one? Is it gold or silver or is it just an ordinary key? Is it rusty or not? What do you do with the key? You can take it, keep it or leave it on the ground. How is the forest: is it the same forest or not? Keep on walking and, in front of you, you will see a brook. How is the brook? Is it small or big? Is it deep or shallow? Is the water cold or warm? Now, you will cross the brook. How do you do that? You can jump over it or wade through it. You can find a bridge or walk on stones that you can see in the brook. Once you have crossed the brook, look at the forest: has it changed or not? What do you see? How do you feel? Keep on walking. Suddenly, in front of you, you will see a house: how is the house? Is it a house you know or not? Is it big or not? Is it old or new? Now, you go in the house. What do you see? How do you feel? Are you comfortable or not? Now, get

---

[37] Demers and Simard (2014) use this daydream for a written exercise. Klippel (1984, p. 82) uses this dream as a trigger for oral practice. As already mentioned, Dortu (1986) wrote a book on induced daydreams in the teaching of French L2.

out of the house and keep on walking in the forest. Has the forest changed or not? Do you see animals, birds, insects? What do you see? Keep on walking. Suddenly, in front of you, you will see a wall. How is the wall: tall or not? Is it thick or not? Is it long or not? Is it made of wood, of bricks or of stones? Is it silver or gold? Visualize the wall as much as you can and try to get to the other side of it. How do you do that? Do you climb or jump over it? Do you try to find a door or the end of the wall? Go over it and look on the other side of the wall. What do you see? Visualize what is on the other side of the wall as well as you can. How do you feel? Visualize what you see and, gradually, open your eyes, because the dream is over.

When the dream is over, the teacher asks every learner to tell his or her dream to the other learners. The teacher can then correct the learners' oral mistakes with the use of gestures as described later in the text. The teacher can also ask questions on the learners' dream or ask a learner to tell the dream of another learner who also told his dream.

At the end of the exercise, the teacher can give a hidden meaning to the words he or she wrote on the board before the exercise. For example:

Forest = The world
Path = The dreamer's life
Key = An important moment with another person
Brook = An important commitment
House = A home
Wall = Death
Over the wall = After death

With that technique, learners will be relaxed, avoid translation, acquire new vocabulary in context, practice the past tenses of the verbs, avoid translation, use many senses and practice their imagination.

With that technique, learners will also practice their listening skills, their speaking skills and their interaction skills.

Teaching the Written Components of the Language

The teaching of the written skills requires a good deal of correction from L2 teachers because even though the main goal of writing is to communicate a written message, more grammar rules have to be mastered than in the oral skills, especially in certain languages such as French and English. When one speaks, one can repeat and explain his or her ideas according to the reactions of people one speaks to. And, of course, that is not the case when one writes; one also has more time to monitor his or her message when one writes than when one speaks.

In many languages such as English and French, the written language differs from the oral language but, with the growing use of the Internet, it is possible that the written code will change in the future and get closer to the oral code. However, for the time being, written and oral codes differ from one another, sometimes a great deal. In general, vocabulary is more sophisticated and grammar rules more complex in the written code than they are in the oral code. Sometimes, there are also many ways to represent in the written code a phoneme of the oral code. In English, for example, the Irish writer George B. Shaw demonstrated that the word fish could be written '*ghoti*' the following way: *gh* as in enou*gh*, *i* as in wom*e*n and *ti* as in na*ti*on. In French, there are also many ways of writing a phoneme: for example, the phoneme o is written as *ô, au, aux, oh, ho, ault, aults, eau, eaux* and so on.

The difference between oral and written codes can also create interferences in the speech of a L2 learner whose L1 alphabet is similar to the L2 one. Indeed, students might then think that because the letters are the same, they should be pronounced the same way which, of course, is not the case: for example, Anglophones learning French L2 often pronounce the final letter of a word, something that is seldom done in French. This can create great confusion in a sentence like *Un homme et une femme* (a man and a woman) that sounds like *Un homme est une femme* (a man is a woman) when the letter *t* is pronounced.[38]

For Aboriginal learners, reading is not a natural process because there is no written tradition in their culture. It is therefore important for the teacher to be patient and to find culturally relevant texts.

Teaching Reading Skills

As already mentioned, in order to acquire a L2 to use Kraschen's terminology, it is absolutely necessary to understand it. The more one understands the more one learns, and that is why reading is so important for learners as long as the texts are not too difficult for them to understand.

---

[38] In French, the letter *t* of the word *est* is pronounced when the word after the word *est* starts with a vowel.

There are many ways to teach reading but all the procedures can be grouped in two categories, intensive and extensive reading procedures: intensive reading is the practice of reading per se and extensive reading is reading for content.

Often, intensive reading implies reading aloud allowing L2 teachers to put the emphasis on the correct pronunciation and also to make a relation between written and oral codes.

For example, at least at the intermediate and advanced levels, the following procedure can be followed.

1. The teacher reads a text aloud while learners read the same text in silence, listening to the teacher;
2. Learners read the text in a low voice opening their mouth and articulating the words;
3. The teacher reads the text aloud again while learners read the text in silence, listening to the teacher;
4. Learners try to understand the new words from the context or using a bilingual dictionary if there is one available;
5. The teacher explains the words learners do not understand, translating them when needed and possible;
6. Every learner reads a part of the text aloud and the teacher corrects his or her pronunciation putting the emphasis on phonemes and relations between the oral and the written codes such as contractions in English or French and liaisons in French;
7. The teacher reads the text aloud once more, but this time faster while learners listen to the teacher without reading the text.

Extensive reading or reading for content implies the use of two types of procedures: skimming and scanning.

Skimming exercises aim at finding, as quickly as possible, the main ideas of a text. For example, learners can be told that, at least in English and French expository prose texts, the important ideas of the text are to be found in the title, introduction, conclusion and the first and last sentences of each paragraph of the text.

Scanning exercises aim at finding specific details of a text such as places, names, dates, etc.

Reading skills can be taught and practiced in many ways and every L2 teacher should create and even invent some because of the importance of reading, a skill learners can also practice on their own. Nevertheless, one should keep in mind that some people just do not like to read and that reading is not characteristic in most Aboriginal cultures. However, as listening is a natural skill in Aboriginal cultures, the teacher can start by reading aloud a text that is culturally relevant for the learners. The learners could be simply asked to listen carefully to the teacher, before they start reading themselves.

Teaching Writing Skills

Writing can also be taught in various ways but, in every writing session, it is important to keep time for preparation and correction.

For the preparation period, after having given the learners different topics, one can proceed as follows.

1. Do a brainstorming activity in which the learners can quickly throw their ideas;
2. Ask learners to pick an idea from what is brainstormed, which becomes a topic for writing;
3. Ask learners to organize the brainstorming ideas starting with the most interesting ones and ending with the less important ones;
4. Ask learners to make a plan of the text they intend to write;
5. Have learners find linking words that they already know or give them linking words they need.

For the correction period, learners should be asked to revise their text, to read the text they wrote many times and to use grammar books, bilingual dictionaries (in the learners' L1 and in the L2 taught) and dictionaries of the L2 they are learning to correct as many mistakes as they can. Correction of learners' mistakes should not be left to the teacher only, because learners have to be able to write by themselves.

Writing is not a part of Aboriginal cultures and therefore, as expository prose is more difficult than literary prose, the teacher could ask the learners to write a poem together.

A good procedure to teach the written skills is the daydream technique. It works well with Aboriginal learners, it is inspired by the radical paradigm and addresses the spiritual aspect of the person: here is an example.

An Induced Daydream: The Beach

The following exercise can be used with intermediate and advanced learners.

The induced daydream described above (i.e. the Forest) could also be used for a writing exercise. Another induced dream is presented below and the L2 teacher can think of a similar induced daydream he or she may like to use with his or her learners.

Before starting the induced dream, the teacher can write on the board a few words and explain them in order to help his or her learners understand better what the teacher says in the dream. For the following daydream, the words written on the board could be: beach, path, cup, boat, sea and hurricane.

The learners sit in a circle while the teacher stands out of the circle and says the following:

> *We will now do an induced daydream. Please sit comfortably, close your eyes and try to visualize the dream I tell you.*
>
> *There is a beach in front of you: how is the beach? Is it big? Is it small? Are you alone on the beach or is the beach crowded? How do you feel? Are you happy? Scared? Is the weather hot, warm or cold? Are you hot, warm or cold? What are you wearing: your regular clothes, your winter clothes or your bathing suit? On the beach, you see a path that goes to the sea. How is the path? Is it long or short? Is it large or narrow? How do you feel? Are you alone or with a friend? Do you have a pet with you? Do you see animals like turtles, lizards or birds on the beach? What do you see. Suddenly, in front of you, you see a cup. How is the cup? Is it big or small? Is it old or new? Is it broken or not? Is it made of plastic, iron, silver or gold? What do you do with the cup? You can kick it, take it with you or leave it there. How do you feel? Is the beach the same as it was at the beginning of the dream? Suddenly, in front of you, you notice a boat on the beach. Visualize the boat as well as you can. Is the boat big or small? Is it an old boat or a new one? What do you do with the boat? You can explore the boat if you wish or simply ignore it. Visualize what you do as well as you can. Keep on walking. You now reach the sea. How is the sea? Is it calm or not? Is the water warm or cold? How do you feel? Are you happy or not? Are you nervous or relaxed? Are you on the same beach or has the beach changed? Visualize the beach as well as you can. Suddenly, there is a hurricane coming? How is the sky? How is the sea? How do you feel? What do you do: you can stay there or hide? Visualize what you see as well as you can. Suddenly, the hurricane disappears, What do you see? Visualize what you see as well as you can. How do you feel? Concentrate on what you see and on how you feel and, gradually, open your eyes, because the daydream is over.*

At the end of the exercise, the teacher can give a hidden meaning to the words he or she wrote on the board before the exercise. For example:

Beach = The world
Path = The dreamer's life
Cup = An important moment with another person
Boat = An important commitment
Sea = A home
Hurricane = Death
After the hurricane = After death

When the dream is over, learners can write first what they saw in their dream – with all details they remember, then discuss it in their composition.

The teacher can also ask questions on the learners' dream or ask a learner to tell, in his or her own words the dream of another learner.

With that technique, learners will be relaxed, avoid translation, acquire new vocabulary in context, practice the past tenses of the verbs, avoid translation, use many senses and practice their imagination.

Lesson Zero

Lesson zero radically differs from other lessons. It is not a L2 lesson per se, but rather a lesson on the teaching and learning procedures the teacher and the learners are engaging in.

Indeed, lesson zero aims at explaining the general design of the course and at motivating and reassuring learners about the learning process they are engaged in and different aspects of their L2 rather than at teaching the L2 as such.

Lesson zero is very useful in creating a strong transactional distance between the teacher and the learners, especially with Aboriginal learners, as already mentioned, and should be given in the learners' L1[39] with illiterate beginners and beginners.

---

[39] If the teacher does not know the learners' L1, another person should give that lesson in the presence of the teacher.

Lesson zero should also be given at the beginning of the program or, even better, before the L2 lessons per se start. After lesson zero, the use of the L1 is not generally encouraged.

Lesson zero is very useful with adults and older teenagers and less useful with younger teenagers and may even be inappropriate with children.

Lesson zero could contain the following elements.

1. Terminal objectives of the program;
2. Learning objects used;
3. Techniques and procedures used;
4. Testing procedures and dates of tests;
5. Skills the program focus on;
6. Class management rules;
7. Course syllabus when appropriate;

For Aboriginal learners, as seen before and whenever possible, it might be relevant to invite an Elder (who was explained the teaching procedures by the teacher) to help give lesson zero in the learners' L1 and to build a strong pedagogical relation between the teacher and learners. The Elder could also perform a smudging ceremony to fill the classroom with positive energy.[40]

Suggested L2 Teaching Procedures

Procedures are sets of organized techniques in which every technique is labeled either as a L2 presentation technique (P) in which learners are presented with new material, a L2 assimilation technique (A) in which learners actually learn the presented material or a L2 use technique (U) in which learners use the material they already know. Those three sets of techniques can be useful for L2 teachers, but one must remember that in the learning process, it could be difficult to distinguish between what is presented, assimilated and used.

Before describing procedures, it is important to remember that, except for real beginners (people with zero knowledge of the L2), most of the time, the traditional differences made in L2 between beginners,

---

[40] Smudging is a traditional Aboriginal ceremony that uses the smoke of sacred plants (such as tobacco, sage, sweet grass, etc.) to create a positive atmosphere.

intermediate and advanced learners are arbitrary. The results of a good placement test are of course very useful but not perfect.

This is why the suggested procedures and techniques described below may have to be adapted to specific Aboriginal learners' needs.

Nevertheless, the suggested procedures and techniques described have all been successfully used by many L2 teachers.

Moreover, every L2 lesson, no matter the students' level, contains the three elements already mentioned: a presentation by the L2 teacher of new material, an appropriation of the new material by learners and the use of known material by learners.

Presentation of new material by the teacher is the most important element of a L2 lesson for illiterate beginners (someone who does not know how to read in his or her L1) and beginners, while the use of known material is the most important element of a L2 lesson for advanced learners. All elements of a L2 lesson for intermediate learners could be of equal importance.

In this book, suggested procedures are given as examples for illiterate beginners, beginners, intermediate and advanced learners.

Procedures for Illiterate Beginners[41]

Teaching a L2 to illiterate teenagers or adults is certainly one of the most challenging tasks L2 teachers may face, because they have to teach a L2 and also literacy.

As it is not possible to do everything at the same time, L2 teachers have to start somewhere.

As the most important skills for L2 learners are listening and speaking, L2 teachers should start with those skills.

The most useful procedures with those learners are the ones of the progressivist and the behaviorist paradigms. L2 teachers can start by

---

[41] At the beginning of every lesson and for every level, it also is important to review what was taught in the previous lesson, to give back students their corrected works, to collect works students did. At the end of every lesson for every level, it is important to summarize what was seen in the lesson and to give homework when appropriate: those tasks are not included in the suggested procedures, but are nevertheless important.

teaching what is the closest to the learners: how to describe themselves and the classroom in their L2. After having mastered how to describe what is here and now, they can be taught what is somewhere else, for example, their homes and families and, using pictures or flash cards what they can find in everyday life: at this stage, using pictures and flash cards provides learners with indispensable clues to comprehension. Later, the L2 teacher can start using verb tenses to allow learners to speak in the future tense and in the past tense: in order to do that, the L2 teacher has to tap on learners' memory and imagination. Gradually, after having started speaking about what is here and now, learners will be able to speak about things that are somewhere else and events that have not happened yet or that already happened.

The following procedure can be used for a three-hour lesson with illiterate beginners.

1. (P) The teacher welcomes the learners;
2. (P) The teacher introduces himself or herself to the learners;
3. (P) With the appropriate gestures, the teacher ask each learner his or her name;
4. (U) Each learner tells the teacher and the whole group his or her name;
5. (P) Using the appropriate gestures, the teacher repeats the names of the learners;
6. (A) Learners, as a group, repeat the names of all the learners;
7. (P) Using the appropriate gestures, the teacher gives L2 words for objects in the classroom;
8. (A) Using the appropriate gestures, learners repeat L2 words for objects in the classroom;
9. (U) Using the appropriate gestures, the teacher asks every learner to name objects in the classroom;
10. (P) Using the appropriate gestures, the teacher gives words and expressions describing the classroom such as '*on your right, on my left, here is, there are* ...';
11. (A) With the appropriate gestures, learners repeat the words and expressions;
12. (U) The teacher asks learners to use those words and expressions in a context and using appropriate gestures;
13. (U) The teacher asks learners to describe the classroom with the appropriate gestures and words.

One must not forget that illiterate beginners cannot understand anything in L2 unless one provides them with specific clues such as actual objects and people. Writing at this level should not be used. Indeed, the emphasis should be put on the oral language and nothing written should be given to the learner before the learner has already learned it orally.

The use of gestures is important with Aboriginal learners, because it helps them understand and acquire basic oral words and expressions and because they can rely on more than two senses (seeing, listening and kinesthetic).

Aboriginal learners at that level would benefit having Elders who speak the L2 coming to class, as soon as they start understanding the oral language.

Procedures for Beginners

As it is the case with illiterate beginners, beginners have very few clues that can help them understand their L2 and that is the reason why it is so important for teachers to use objects that are in the classroom as well as pictures of everyday objects and life with those learners.

It is also important to reeducate their ear because they are not used to discriminate L2 phonemes that do not exist in their L1, as it will be discussed later.

The suggested procedure for a three-hour lesson for beginners is as follows.

1. (P) The teacher says '*hi*';
2. (A) The whole class repeats '*hi*';
3. (A) Every learner repeats '*hi*';
4. (P) With the appropriate gesture, the teacher says '*My name is ...* ';
5. (P) The teacher makes sure that every learner understands what the words mean;
6. (A) With the appropriate gestures, every learner says '*My name is ...* ' and gives his or her name;
7. (P) The teacher indicates a learner and says '*His (or her) name is...*';
8. (A) The teacher asks another learner what the first learner's name is;
9. (A) With the appropriate gestures, the designated learner says the first learner's names;

10. (P) The teacher repeats '*His (or her) name is ...* ';
11. (P) The teacher asks '*Who is he (or she)?*';
12. (P) The teacher makes sure that every learner understands the question;
13. (A) The whole class repeats '*Who is he (or she)?*';
14. (A) Every learner repeats the question and the teacher corrects their pronunciation when needed;
15. (P) The teacher points at an object in the classroom and says '*This is ...* ';
16. 15-(P) The teacher says '*What is this?*';
17. (A) The whole class says '*This is ...* ';
18. (A) Every learner repeats '*This is ...* ' and the teacher corrects the learners' pronunciation when needed, congratulating them when it is good;
19. (A) The teacher does the same thing for every object in the classroom;
20. (P) Gradually and with the appropriate gestures, the teacher introduces new structures to describe the classroom such as '*on my right, on your right, on my left ....*';
21. (P) The teacher makes sure that every learner understands the structures;
22. (A) With the appropriate gestures, the whole class repeats all the structures;
23. (A) Every learner repeats structures and the teacher corrects their pronunciation, congratulating them when it is good;
24. (U) With the appropriate gestures, a few learners describe the classroom;
25. (A) With the appropriate gestures, the whole class repeats words and structures practiced orally;
26. (A) Every learner repeats a few words and sentences and the teacher corrects their pronunciation, congratulating them when it is good;
27. (P) The teacher writes on the board words and structures practiced orally;
28. (P) The teacher reads what is written on the board and the whole class repeats;
29. (A) Learners read what is written on the board;
30. (A) A few learners read what is written on the board;
31. (U) The teacher divides the class in small groups;

32. (U) Every group choses a learner who will ask the other learners of the group questions seen in class.
33. (U) Learners work in small groups, asking questions and giving answers practiced orally in class;
34. (U) Every group shows the rest of the class what they did in their group;
35. (A) The teacher congratulates every group;
36. (A) The teacher repeats one more time words and structures practiced orally in the lesson.

The suggested procedure may seem too simple and even trivial but, for beginners, it implies a lot of energy to try to understand, repeat, memorize and use words and structures they have never practiced orally before, as anyone who once took a course to learn a totally unknown language can testify. For teachers, it also implies a lot of preparation, energy, listening and patience, because otherwise, learners may get discouraged.

Moreover, the suggested procedure does not use translation.

With Aboriginal learners, the use of gestures is important because, as mentioned above, with gestures, they can rely on more senses.

As with the illiterate beginners, Aboriginal learners of this level would benefit having Elders who speak the L2 coming to class, as soon as they start understanding the oral language

Before introducing the written code, the teacher must make sure that all the written material has already been mastered orally by the learners. With Aboriginal learners, that is even more important, because writing is not part of most Aboriginal cultures.

Before they start writing, learners must have read the material.

Most of the time, the proposed procedures works well with illiterate beginners and beginners but not all the time as the following testimony shows.

Testimony 21: When Students Repeat without Understanding

The following event happened in the Montréal area.

"I teach French L2 to real beginners, adult Vietnamese who speak Chinese as their L1. I begin my lesson as I always do with 'Bonjour, je m'appelle Pierre (Good morning! I am Pierre)'.

Without me asking anything or even uttering a word or making a gesture, the whole class repeats what could sound like 'Bonjour, je m'appelle Pierre (Good

morning! I am Pierre)'. I am puzzled because I was not expecting such a reaction. Usually, students listen to me and repeat only when asked. Pointing at myself, I say 'I ... am Pierre'. All learners, pointing at themselves, they repeat 'Je m'appelle Pierre (I ... am Pierre)'.

As I do not know neither their L1 nor specific gestures of their culture, I cannot communicate with them whatsoever and have to ask an interpreter for the first lessons to make sure my students understand simple words and, most important, the procedure I use to teach them."

Procedures for Intermediate Learners

With intermediate learners, we do not need an interpreter to communicate with learners in their L2, although it may sometimes take a lot of imagination, patience, gestures and appropriate learning objects.

At that level, it is important to motivate learners: for example, they need L2 material appropriate to their linguistic needs and specific interests, material that can be difficult to find on the market, unless the teacher adapts or creates his or her own material.

With adolescent and adult learners, it is important for L2 teachers to explain to their learners that language learning is a cyclical rather than a linear process and that, therefore, it is normal for them to make mistakes and even often the same mistakes over and over again, even though they know they are mistakes: they might be under the impression that they are not learning much; children, however, may not need to be told that.

At a certain point of the L2 learning process, although it is difficult to know exactly when, there is a qualitative shift in the learners' L2 knowledge and, almost all of a sudden, their skills are improved. However, the days and even weeks before that qualitative shift happens can be very discouraging: that is the reason why learners have to be made aware of the fact that it is normal to feel discouraged and that they simply have to keep on working and practicing their L2.

Sometimes, however, some intermediate learners simply stop improving, most likely because, in their opinion, they know their L2 well enough to meet their needs: indeed, some leaners may not need to become advanced learners.

Nevertheless, it is always important for L2 teachers to listen to their learners for two reasons: first of all, to understand what they say or are trying to say, but also to identify mistakes they make and keep on making

Procedures for Intermediate Learners

and, gradually, to correct those mistakes. Listening to learners takes time, patience and constant attention, but it is crucial in the learning process.

For a three-hour class for intermediate learners, the following procedure can be used.

1. (U) The teacher asks learners to describe their weekend, what they did yesterday or after the last class, starting with the best learners[42];
2. (U) The teacher listens to every learner;
3. (A) The teacher asks the other learners to listen carefully to the learner who is speaking[43];
4. (A) The teacher asks a learner to summarize what the learner who spoke said;
5. (U) The teacher divides the class in small groups;
6. (U) The teacher asks every group to prepare a sketch on a topic chosen by the teacher or the learners;
7. (U) The learners work as a group in their L2
8. (U) The teacher gives groups enough time to prepare their sketch;
9. (U) Every group plays their sketch in front of the class;
10. (A) The other learners listen carefully to every sketch;
11. (A) The teacher asks a learner to summarize the sketch of a group she or he is not a part of;
12. (P) The teacher reads aloud a text of a level appropriate to the learners' level;
13. (P) The teacher explains new words and structures;
14. (A) Learners read the text in a low voice;
15. (A) Every learner reads a part of the text aloud, starting with the best learners;
16. (A) When a learner has read his or her part of the text aloud, the teacher reads the same part aloud;
17. (A) When the whole text has been read aloud by learners, the teacher reads the text aloud.

At that level, Aboriginal learners would benefit having in class an Aboriginal author who writes in the L2.

---

[42] Starting with the best learners allow other learners to practice their listening skills and learn new words, expressions and speaking strategies.
[43] When learners are able to listen carefully to one another, they can learn from one another.

Procedures for Advanced Learners

L2 teaching to advanced learners requires excellent L2 skills, a thorough knowledge of its grammar, as well as of the required teaching techniques and procedures. Advanced learners can ask (and most of the time do) specific questions about the L2 grammar. As many of those questions come from the perspective of their L1 and the comparison they make between their L1 and L2, answering them can be problematic for many L2 teachers. For example, it is very difficult to explain to English L1 learners how to use French past tenses of verbs or to explain to French L1 learners how to use English prepositions.

Moreover, L2 teaching techniques and procedures for advanced learners are more similar to L1 teaching techniques and procedures to the point that, with very advanced learners, they can be virtually identical. A few very advanced learners even switch to another L1, their prior L1 becoming their L2 and their prior L2 becoming their L1.

For a three-hour lesson, the following procedure can be used.

1. (P) Learners listen to the news;
2. (P) The teacher repeats and explains new words and structures of the news;
3. (A) A learner summarizes the news;
4. (U) Learners give their opinion about topics of the news;
5. (A) The teacher divides the class in small groups;
6. (A) The teacher gives every group a different expository prose text (like a an article in a newspaper);
7. (A) Learners read the texts, underline new words and expressions, trying to find their meaning from the context or with the use of dictionaries;
8. (A) A learner from every group summarizes the text the group read;
9. (P) The teacher gives the learners all the texts;
10. (P) The teacher explains new words and structures;
11. (A) The teacher reads one of the texts aloud;
12. (U) Learners write a short text in which they give their opinion about one of the texts.

It is important to notice here again that the three sets of techniques (presentation (P), appropriation (A), and use (U)) are very closely linked together and are sometimes very hard to distinguish one from another

Procedures for Advanced Learners

because L2 learning is a cyclical process. However, they are grouped here to help L2 teachers better understand the suggested procedures.

At that level Aboriginal learners will benefit having an Aboriginal politician who speaks the L2 invited to the class.

Table 3 illustrates how suggested procedures relate to the four students' levels referred to in this chapter

Tab. 3: Relations between Learners' Linguistic Levels and Elements of Procedures

Illiterate beginners	Presentation +++	Assimilation+	Use - -
Beginners	Presentation ++	Assimilation +	Use -
Intermediate learners	Presentation +	Assimilation +	Use +
Advanced learners	Presentation -	Assimilation +	Use ++

(Elements change according to levels: the + sign means that we must focus on this element while the '-' sign means that we do not have to focus on this element).

Chapter 7:
After Teaching Procedures

Correction of Errors

The way an error (or a mistake, for that matter) is seen greatly depends of the L2 paradigm in which the lesson is given.

In the classical, progressivist and behaviorist paradigms, errors are referred to as mistakes because those paradigms focus more on the code than on the message. A mistake is something the L2 teacher wishes his or her learners to avoid as much as possible and, often, L2 learners also want to avoid mistakes by speaking and writing as less as possible, a sure way not to make mistakes.

With Aboriginal learners, the teacher has to be careful not to hurt their self-esteem when correcting their errors.

Indeed, in the classical, progressivist and behaviorist paradigms, teachers often discourage their learners by correcting their mistakes all the time, as illustrated in the following testimony.

Testimony 22: When the L2 Teacher's Corrections Discourage the Learners

The following event happened in the Montréal area.
"I can still remember papers we had written a L2 professor would give back to us full of corrections in red ink and the shyness we all felt when he would give us our marks aloud in front of everybody and to which he would also add his negative comments. We had to write at least one paper a week and every week, he would do that and it was always painful for us. The way he corrected our papers was very discouraging for us and it was not helping us to learn the L2 he was teaching."

In the communicative and radical paradigms however, errors are more tolerated because they are seen as integral components of the L2 learning process: after all, it is quite normal and natural to make errors when learning something as complex as a L2.

There are two types of errors: errors coming from the interference of the L1 with the L2 and errors coming from the learning of a specific L2 itself.

Errors coming from the learning of a specific L2 itself are errors almost every learner makes learning that specific language whether as a L1 or as a L2.

When learning French for example, many learners, Francophones or not, use the conditional instead of the imperfect after the word '*si*' and it is common to hear '*si j'aurais (if I would have)*' instead of '*si j' avais (If I had)*'.

In English, as explained by Krashen (1981), the morpheme 's' (that indicates the plural of most words as well as the complement of a noun among other things) is acquired or mastered in the same fashion by almost every English learner the world over including Anglophones.

Errors coming from the interference between a L1 and a L2 are specific to learners sharing the same L1 and who are learning the same L2 such as Francophones learning English or Anglophones learning French. Those errors are highly predictable by someone who knows learners' L1 and L2.[44]

Although normal and part of the language appropriation process, errors have to be corrected whenever possible because otherwise, they can become fossilized over the time and very difficult to correct.

To correct errors, however, requires a lot of tact on the teachers' part because, as mentioned earlier, harsh correction can lead to speech or writing avoidance by the learners.

Of course, as a teacher cannot correct all the errors at the same time, he or she will have to choose the errors to be corrected: errors blocking the communication process must be corrected first. For example, Anglophones learning French will often say '*Je sens mauvais (I smell bad)*' instead of '*Je me sens mal (I feel bad)*' when they wish to say that they do not feel good, reproducing in their L2 a L1 structure: this type of error will undoubtedly create confusion among French speakers who might even start laughing, and it must be corrected as soon as possible.

---

[44] See Allain (1996).

Errors like that can be corrected as long as they are recognized and explained. When all the learners feel comfortable, they can even start laughing when they make them.

That is especially true with Aboriginal learners who, in general, like to have a good laugh.

Demers and Bérubé (1995, 1996) suggest an oral error correction strategy based on the use of specific gestures that can be highly effective and fun. The procedure is as follows.

Oral Error Correction with the Help of Gestures

Using gestures is first aimed at helping learners be aware that they made an error. Moreover, using specific gestures aims at helping learners recognize the type of errors they made, as well as developing strategies to correct themselves without interrupting the communication flow or disturbing the class atmosphere.

When teaching a L2, the teacher can proceed as follows.[45]

1. The gesture one makes to tell a car driver to back up indicates that the learner must use a past tense;
2. The gesture one makes to tell a car driver to move forward indicates that the learner must use a future tense or a conditional;
3. The gesture one makes to tell someone to go faster indicates to the learner to speak faster;
4. By pointing to his or her ear, the teacher indicates to the learner to speak louder;
5. A swaying of the hand indicates to the learner to use the right word order;
6. The flickering of the middle finger indicates to the learner to add a word such as a preposition or a conjunction;
7. A disjointed gesture with the hand tells the learner to keep on talking;
8. A circular gesture with the index tells the learner to explain an idea one more time;
9. The gesture used to indicate that the food is good tells the learner that he or she did well or avoided a common error. This encouraging

---

[45] The suggested gestures' meaning is understood by English and French Canadians.

gesture is always welcome by learners and the teacher should use it as often as possible.

The suggested procedure may seem complicated but, after a little practice with learners, it is amazing to see how quickly they understand what each gesture means. Gestures can vary from one teacher to another (and from one culture to another), but the goal should always be to help learners to correct their own errors and to gradually develop a linguistic sense[46] that will eventually prevent them from making constant errors.

The gestures technique proposed above belongs to the radical paradigm and works well with all learners. With Aboriginal learners however, we have to be very explicit as to the reason why we use it, because otherwise they might be a little frightened by so many gestures: indeed, in their C1, Aboriginals do not make many gestures when they speak as already mentioned.

Writing Error Correction

When writing, learners have more time to formulate their ideas and, in theory, should not make as many errors as when speaking. However, generally, this is not the case maybe because of the difficulties of the written code.

As with oral error correction, the aim of writing error correction is to enable learners to write by themselves without making errors and that is why learners should have access to grammars and dictionaries, computers and the Internet as long as they know how to use them.

Instead of correcting learners' errors, the teacher may simply indicate the errors and the types of errors they made: for example, verb errors, word order errors, orthographical errors, lexical errors, missing words and so forth and so on. That way, learners will have a chance to correct themselves and learn how to write by themselves.

Teachers should not forget that learners' autonomy is the main goal of error correction and that by correcting all their mistakes, they are not helping them to reach that goal.

---

[46] See Sapir (1970).

Phonetic Correction

There are many ways to do phonetic correction but they all require from teachers a sound knowledge of L2 phonology (the set of phonemes pertaining to a specific language) and, whenever possible, of the learners' L1 phonology.

Often, phonetic correction can be done in a language laboratory where learners work on their own using appropriate softwares.

The teacher can also use IPA (International Phonetic Alphabet[47]) symbols, asking learners to repeat phonemes of the L2, all together at first and then individually.

The teacher can also use phonetics per se by describing how phonemes are produced by different organs (tongue, teeth, palate, soft palate …). The use of phonetics can be very useful and even indispensable when teaching a L2 that differs a great deal from the learner's L1 such as English L2 or French L2 to L1 speakers of Mandarin, Tamil, Hindi, etc.

The teacher can also use verbotonal phonetics: this correction technique assumes that, because L2 learners are not able to hear specific L2 phonemes that do not exist in their L1, they cannot reproduce them.

Therefore, verbotonal phonetics aims at reeducating the learner's ear so that he or she can actually hear L2 unfamiliar sounds.

Using all the techniques of verbotonal phonetics requires exhaustive knowledge of L1 and L2 phonologies but some of its techniques, such as those described below, are quite simple and most of the time highly effective.

Basics of Verbotonal Phonetics

Verbotonal Phonetics, as already mentioned, aims at reeducating the learners' auditive perceptions in order for them to discriminate sounds that they do not use in their L1 and that they have to use in the L2 they are learning.

---

[47] As mentioned earlier, IPA was introduced in 1888 by the IPA Association: its goal is to provide written symbols for all existing phonemes for every language. Many dictionaries provide those symbols for a specific language.

Verbotonal phonetics was widely used with the structure-global methods of the sixties of the last century. The structure-global methods belong to the behaviorist paradigm and are partly based on the Gestalt psychology. For the Gestalt psychology, human perceptions greatly depends on the background knowledge of individuals. For example, to recognize a song they already know, people do not have to listen to the entire song: the first notes will trigger the whole song. New songs however do not trigger the background knowledge of individuals, because there is no background knowledge. In fact, background knowledge can lead to false perceptions when, for example, the first notes of two different melodies are identical while the rest of the melodies differ.

When the communicative paradigm emerges, many L2 teachers stopped using verbotonal phonetics, because they were now focusing on the message and no longer on the form of the communication process.

The following exercises help learners to perceive phonemes of the L2 they are learning that do not exist in their L1.

1. The teacher whispers words learners have problems to reproduce: when one whispers, usual distinctions between voiced and voiceless consonant sounds (for example, *b* versus *p* or *d* versus *t*) are changed and learners may then be able to reproduce phonemes they usually cannot reproduce;
2. The teacher cuts long words or word groups in smaller units, first starting with the beginning of words or word groups and then starting with the end of words or word groups and have learners repeat the smaller units: that way, learners might be able to more easily reproduce common contractions and liaisons encountered in the spoken language;
3. The teacher uses his or her fingers to beat the rhythm of long words or word groups: as every language has a specific rhythm which has a great impact on its pronunciation, being able to reproduce that rhythm helps improving pronunciation;
4. The teacher pronounces a specific phoneme a little different than its regular pronunciation in such a way that learners can hear it better: for example, it is easier for Anglophones to hear the French u in a word like '*étudiant (student)*' than it is in a word like '*rue (street)*'. However, using this technique requires a thorough knowledge of L2 phonology and a sound knowledge of students' L1.

Correcting pronunciation errors is important and can also be a lot of fun: in fact, it is very useful in the creation of an optimal transactional distance because it lowers anxiety.

In progressivist and behaviorist paradigms, students' L2 pronunciation has to be as close as possible to native's L1 pronunciation. However, in communicative and radical paradigms and at least in the case of very widely spoken languages where there is no standardized way to pronounce (such as English with all its different accents), teachers have to focus on pronunciation errors that mislead or break communication.

Testing

Scientific testing is a rather recent technique in L2 didactics, going back only to the behaviorist paradigm. Before that, teachers and professors would evaluate their L2 students' performance in a subjective way as Madsen (1983, p. 5) says:

> Testing during the last century and the early decades of this one[48] was basically intuitive or subjective and dependant on the personal impressions of teachers.

There are various procedures for language testing according to the goals of testing, the L2 methods used and the time that can be devoted to testing.

According to the general goals of testing, a distinction is made between formative and summative evaluations: formative testing is used when one needs to know learners' levels in order to find adequate teaching material for instance, while summative testing is used to mark learners.

Placement tests are used to create homogenous groups of learners and also to verify if candidates have appropriate L2 skills for a job, for example.

According to specific methods, L2 tests are discrete or holistic. Discrete or objective tests can be used with approaches focusing on linguistic forms while holistic or global tests can be used with approaches focusing on message.[49]

---

[48] Madsen is referring to the nineteenth and twentieth centuries.
[49] For more details, see Demers (1994).

Classical, progressivist and behaviorist methods generally use discrete tests while communicative and radical methods usually use holistic tests.

Discrete tests usually take shorter time to administer and correct but their design takes longer and statistical measures such as validity and reliability must be determined.

Among discrete tests, there are multiple choice tests, fill in the blank tests and self-evaluation questionnaires, for example. Today, most of those tests can be administered at a distance in synchronous (real) or asynchronous (virtual) time.

Among holistic tests, there are interviews and compositions or essays.

Holistic tests take into account elements that cannot be measured by discrete tests such as gestures and oral interaction in interviews and rhetoric (organization of ideas) in essays. However, they can be time consuming and their correction can be subjective unless at least three people correct them.

Except for interviews that have to be done in a synchronous mode, holistic tests can be administered in synchronous and asynchronous modes.

Holistic tests require a grid in order to evaluate different components of the learner's performances.

When evaluating interviews for instance, the following components could be taken into account:

1. Vocabulary;
2. Grammar;
3. Gestures;
4. Pronunciation;
5. Oral comprehension;
6. Fluency;
7. Interaction.

When evaluating essays, the following components could be taken into account:

1. Precision of vocabulary;
2. Richness of vocabulary;
3. Orthography;
4. Syntax;

5. Punctuation;
6. Rhetoric.

Testing is not a part of traditional Aboriginal teaching and Aboriginal learners do not like this aspect of eurocentric pedagogy.

Often, Aboriginal learners will even avoid coming to class when there is a test scheduled. As testing is an important component of most L2 programs, the L2 teacher must explain what the goals of testing are and why it can be important and useful for all learners, including Aboriginal learners.

In order to lower the Aboriginal learner's stress and fear of being tested, the L2 teacher could practice quizzes and tests with his or her learners on a regular basis and always give quick feedback of quizzes and tests to Aboriginal learners. That feedback should be done on an individual basis and the emphasis should always be put on the positive aspects of the results.

Conclusion

L2 teaching cannot be learned by taking L2 didactics courses or reading specialized literature only.

Though studying and passing L2 didactics courses are important steps prior to L2 teaching, L2 teaching cannot be learned by taking L2 didactics courses or reading specialized literature only.

To possess a thorough knowledge of the L2 being taught, to establish an optimal transactional distance with the learners, to master L2 teaching techniques and to use appropriate learning objects may be seen as L2 teaching cornerstones, but all those things can be learned only by teaching.

In this book, important L2 concepts were defined, eurocentric paradigms used today in L2 didactics were described, traditional Aboriginal teaching techniques were explained and common L2 practices were given.

The emphasis was put on L2 teaching to Aboriginal learners. The suggested techniques that are described for Aboriginal learners can also be used with non-Aboriginal learners.

Indeed, traditional Aboriginal techniques could have positive impacts on language teaching and language didactics as well.

L2 didactics is constantly evolving and the actual and unprecedented globalization that impacts on languages and cultures will most likely increase L2 didactics evolution.

Indeed, if the interest in learning major world languages such as English, Mandarin, Russian, French, Spanish or Arabic is rising, learning and reviving minority languages such as Basque, Cree or Gaelic is also rising and more and more people will want to learn at least one L2.

Moreover, as recent technological developments now allows L2 distance education, for example, something that was difficult until fairly recently, it is not difficult to imagine that even newer technologies such as virtual reality or holograms will also impact on L2 teaching and learning in the next future.

However, if new technologies will most likely profoundly change L2 teaching and learning, it is also most likely that new techniques from the radical paradigm such as the use of suggestion and even hypnosis will bring profound changes to L2 teaching as well.

As the use of an artificial language designed to help human beings communicate such as Esperanto has not been successful in the past and because it is very improbable that all nations would agree to use a same language as a means of communication, it is only by learning at least one L2 that people all over the world will be able to communicate and interact. This will be possible if our knowledge and practice of L2 didactics keep on evolving and if L2 teachers keep abreast of most recent discoveries in the field.

As explained before, learning a dominant L2, such as English, French or Spanish can be perceived as a threat by Aboriginal learners because they experience acculturation and the L2 teacher has to be aware of that. Indeed, if the L2 teacher cannot change the L2 he or she is teaching, the teacher can teach it in an unthreatening way. To do that, the teacher has to create a strong pedagogical relationship with the learners.

Moreover, the use of Aboriginal learning objects is also a good way to lower the threat and the stress of Aboriginal learners. However, using learning objects belonging to Aboriginal cultures might be seen as going against regular L2 teaching, because L2 teachers are used to link the L2 they teach to the L2 culture: for example, it is normal for an English L2 teacher to use English songs, English newspapers, movies, etc. When teaching Aboriginal learners however, L2 teachers have to use cultural elements that belong to Aboriginal cultures rather than cultural elements that belong to the L2 they teach.

References

Allain, A. (1995). Les apports de l'analyse contrastive dans un cours de français langue seconde. In Pellerin, S. (Ed.). *La Didactique du français L2 dans les universités et collèges canadiens*. Montréal: ACEFNU – FCLE.

Allain, A. and P. Demers. (2016). Introduction. In Allain, A. and P. Demers (Eds.). *Recherche et enseignement en milieu autochtone, La Revue de l'AQEFLS*, 32(1): pp. 5–10.

Allain, A., P. Demers and F. Pelletier. (2013). Pour un enseignement efficace des langues aux Autochtones. In Lévesque, C., E. Cloutier and D. Salée (Eds.). *Cahiers DIALOG no 2013–03. Actes du Colloque La co-construction des connaissances en contexte autochtone: cinq études de cas*: pp. 7–23. Available online (Link retrieved on August 20, 2019): https://docplayer.fr/16337008-La-coconstruction-des-connaissances-en-contexte-autochtone-cinq-etudes-de-cas.html.

Allain, A., P. Demers, G. Grigoroiu and F. Pelletier. (2017). Pour un enseignement efficace du français aux Autochtones du Québec. In *Bulletin de l'AQEFLS 36ième congrès*. Available online (Link retrieved on June 24, 2019 under *Reflets* Demers 2017): http://aqefls.org/aqeflsintranet/programme_detaille_public.php?an=2017.

Bateson, G. et al. (1981). *La nouvelle communication*. Seuil: Paris.

Battiste, M. (2002). *Indigenous Knowledge and Pedagogy in First Nations Education: A Literature Review with Recommendations*. Online document (Link retrieved on June 24, 2019): https://www.afn.ca/uploads/files/education/24._2002_oct_marie_battiste_indigenousknowledgeandpedagogy_lit_review_for_min_working_group.pdf.

Berlitz, M. (1897). *The Berlitz Method for Teaching Modern Languages*. Leipzig: Siegfried Cronbach.

Bertrand, Y. 1998. *Théories contemporaines de l'éducation*. Lyon: Chronique Sociale; Montréal: Éditions Nouvelles.

Bérubé, G. and P. Demers. (1995). Correction of Speech Errors: Some Suggestions. In Duquette, G. (Ed.). *Second Language Practice-Classroom Strategies for Developing Communicative Competence*. Available online (Link retrieved on

March 4, 2021): https://books.google.ca/books?id=YQJXzy4pGnMC&pg=PA108&lpg=PA108&dq=b%C3%A9rub%C3%A9+guylaine+pierre+demers+article&source=bl&ots=WJB4JuNaS_&sig=ACfU3U3NESgwyhvf9YBK7k6_i5dG9m-uiA&hl=fr&sa=X&ved=2ahUKEwj3uIKv8Zbv AhUKFFkFHdVPDwAQ6AEwEnoECBAQAw#v=onepage&q=b%C3%A9rub%C3%A9%20guylaine%20pierre%20demers%20article&f=false.

Bess, H. (1992). *Méthodes et pratiques des manuels de langue.* Paris: Didier.

Birdwhistell, R. (1960). *Kinesics and Context.* Philadelphia: UPP.

Campeau, D. (2016). Valeurs autochtones en salle de classe: recours à la pédagogie autochtone et à la pédagogie du lieu pour favoriser une interface culturelle. In Allain, A. and P. Demers (Eds.). *Recherche et enseignement en milieu autochtone, La Revue de l'AQEFLS,* 32 (1): pp. 23–40.

Caravolas. (1994). *La didactique des langues Précis d'histoire, 1450–1700.* Montréal: PUM.

Chabot, D. and M. Chabot. (2005). *Pédagogie émotionnelle.* Victoria: Trafford.

Chartrand, R. (2016). *Running Head: Redefining Education Through Anishinaabe Pedagogy.* Online document (Link retrieved on June 24, 2019): https://mspace.lib.umanitoba.ca/bitstream/handle/1993/31755/Chartrand.Rebecca.pdf?sequence=1&isAllowed=y.

Chomsky, N. (1957). *Syntactic Structure.* Mouton: The Hague.

Clottes, J. and D. Lewis-Williams. (2001). *Les chamanes de la préhistoire.* Paris: La maison des roches.

Commission de vérité et réconciliation du Canada. (2012). *Le Canada, les peuples autochtones et les pensionnats Ils sont venus pour les enfants.*Available online (Link retreived on April 3, 2021 : Read - Ils sont venus pour les enfants : Le Canada, les peuples autochtones et les pensionnats: Commission de vérité et réconciliation du Canada - desLibris

Conseil de l'Europe. (2019). *Le Cadre européen commun de référence pour les langues.* Online (Link retrieved on June 16, 2019): https://rm.coe.int/16802fc3a8.

Cuq, J.-P. and I. Gruca. (2018). *Cours de didactique du français langue étrangère et seconde.* Grenoble: PUG.

Cyrulnik, B. (2000). *Les Nourritures Affectives.* Paris: Odile Jacob.

Demers, P. (1990). *Apport des connaissances d'un domaine spécifique à la compréhension orale en français L2 d'étudiants anglophones adultes de niveau intermédiaire.* Thèse de doctorat non publiée.

Demers, P. (1992). La compréhension orale en langue seconde constitue-elle un nouveau paradigme? In *Acquisition et enseignement/apprentissage des langues.* Grenoble: LIDILEM – Université Stendhal – Grenoble III.

Demers, P. (1994). Evaluation and Second Language Learning in Second Language Service-Advanced Education and Labor-Government of New Brunswick. *Ensemble,* 4(1): pp. 1–4.

Demers, P. (1996). The Use of Hypnosis in L2 Acquisition. In Pellerin, S. (Ed.). *La Didactique du français L2 dans les universités et collèges canadiens.* Montréal: ACEFNU – FCLE.

Demers, P. (2008). *Second and Foreign Language Didactics: Theoretical and Practical Considerations.* Victoria: Trafford.

Demers, P. and G. Bérubé. (1995). Correction of Speech Errors: Some Suggestions. In Duquette, G. (Ed.). *Second Language Practice.* Clevedon: Multilingual Matters.

Demers, P. and G. Bérubé. (1996). La correction gestuelle des erreurs de production linguistique orale en L2. In Pellerin, S. (Ed.). *La Didactique du français L2 dans les universités et collèges canadiens.* Montréal: ACEFNU – FCLE.

Demers, P. and J. Simard (2015). Présentation de quelques techniques propres à l'enseignement traditionnel autochtone et exemple concret d'application de celles-ci dans l'enseignement du français écrit à une clientèle autochtone adulte dans une perspective langue seconde. In *Revue de la persévérance et de la réussite scolaires chez les Premiers Peuples vol.1.* Available online (Link retrieved on June 24, 2019): http://nikanite.uqac.ca/revue/Perseverance_et_reussite_scolaires_2014/FLASH/data/77.html.

Demers, P., A. Pardo and F. Pelletier. (2005). Prototype of an Online French as a Second Language Course. *Distances,* 7(2). Link retrieved on May 26, 2020: http://distances.teluq.ca/wp-content/uploads/2019/03/Prototype-of-an-online-course-french-as-a-second-language.pdf.

Dickason, O. (1996). *Les Premières Nations du Canada.* Sillery: Septentrion.

Dortu, J. (1986). *Une classe de rêve.* Paris: Clé.

Drury, N. (1989). *The Elements of Human Potential.* Dorset: Element Books Ltd.

Dufeu, B. (1994). *Teaching Myself.* Oxford: Oxford University Press.

Elias, J. and S. Merriam (1983). *Penser l'éducation des adultes.* Montréal: Guérin.

First Nations' Pedagogy online (n.d.). Link retrieved on July 11, 2019: https://firstnationspedagogy.ca/circletalks.html.

Freire, P. (1996). *Pedagogy of the Oppressed.* New York: Continuum.

Galisson, R. (1983). *La Suggestion dans l'enseignement.* Paris: Clé.

Gatti, M. (2009). *Littérature amérindienne au Québec.* Montréal: Bibliothèque québécoise.

Gauthier, C. and D. Jeffrey (Eds.) (1999). *Enseigner et séduire.* Québec: Les Presses de l'Université Laval.

Gélinas, C. (2013). La représentation des Autochtones depuis le contact. In Beaulieu, A., S. Gervais and M. Papillon (Ed.). *Les Autochtones et le Québec.* Montréal: PUM.

Germain, C. (1993). *Le point sur l'approche communicative en didactique des langues.* Montréal: CEC.

Giura, A. et al. (1980). The effects of benzodiazepine (Valium) on permeability of ego boundaries. *Language Learning,* 30: pp. 351–363.

Gollan, G. and M. Byrn. (2012). Becoming a Culturally Competent Teacher. In Beresford, Q., G. Partington, and G. Gower (Eds.). *Reform and Resistance in Aboriginal Education. Revised Edition,* pp. 379–402. Crawley: University of Western Australia Publishing.

Gollan, S. and M. Malin. (2012). Teachers and Families Working Together to Build Stronger Features for Our Children in Schools. In Beresford, Q., G. Partington and G. Gower (Eds.). *Reform and Resistance in Aboriginal Education. Revised Edition*: pp. 149–173. Crawley: University of Western Australia Publishing.

Government of Canada. (2018) *National Inquiry into Missing and Murdered Indigenous Women and Girls-Executive Summary of the Final Report.* Report available online (Link retrieved on July 9, 2019): https://www.mmiwg-ffada.ca/wp-ontent/uploads/2019/06/Executive_Summary.pdf.

Government of Canada. (2020). *Indigenous Languages Act.* Ottawa: Minister of Justice.

Graveline, G. (1996). *Circle as Pedagogy: Aboriginal Tradition Enacted in a University Classroom.* Unpublished Ph.D. dissertation, Dalhousie University.

Grigoroiu, G. (2016). Tradition orale et vision du monde autochtone: la narration orale, une pratique interculturelle d'expression et d'apprentissage partagé. In Allain, A. and P. Demers (Eds.). *Recherche et enseignement en milieu autochtone, La Revue de l'AQEFLS*, 32(1): pp. 59–75.

Groff, S. (1992). *Royaumes de l'inconscient humain*. Paris: Du Rocher.

Groff, S. (2000). *Psychology of the Future: Lessons from Modern Consciousness Research*. Albany: SUNY Press.

Guberina, P. (1964). The audio visual global and structural method. In Libbish, B. (Ed.). *Advances in the Teaching of Modern Languages*. Volume 1. Oxford: Pergammon.

Hall, E. (1959). *The Silent Language*. New York: Doubleday.

Hall, E. (1966). *The Hidden Dimension*. New York: Doubleday.

Hammerly, H. (1989). *French Immersion: Myths and Reality*. Calgary: Detselig Enterprises Ltd.

Hammerman, M. (1979). Hypnosis and Language Learning. *Eric Document*. ED 181 741.

Her Majesty the Queen in Right of Canada. (2021). English and French: Towards a Substantive Equality of Official languages of Canada. White Paper. Catalogue number: CH14-50/2021E-PDF.

Houssaye, J. (1987). *École et vie active*. Paris: Delachaux et Niestlé.

Howatt, A. with H. Widdowson. (2004). *A History of English Language Teaching*. Oxford: Oxford University Press.

Ignace, M. (2016). *First Nations Language Curriculum Building Guide*. West Vancouver: First Nations Education Steering Committee and First Nations Schools Association. PDF Available online (Link retrieved on March 1, 2021): 614108-FNESC-LANGUAGE-BULDING-CURRICULUM-BOOK-290316-B-F-with-Cover.pdf (fnsa.ca)

Joseph, B. (2013). What is an Aboriginal Medecine Wheel? In *Indigenous Corporate Training Inc*. p. 1. Site (Link retrieved on July 9, 2019): https://www.ictinc.ca/blog/what-is-an-aboriginal-medicine-wheel.

Joyce, B. and M. Weil. (1996). *Models of Teaching*. Boston: Allyn and Bacon.

Knowles, M. (1980). *The Modern Practice of Adult Education*. New York: Cambridge.

Kapesh, A. (2019). *Eukuan nin matshi-manitu Innushkueu Je suis une maudite Sauvagesse*. Montréal: Mémoire d'encrier.

Klippel, F. (1984). *Keep Talking: Fluency Activities for Language Teaching*. Cambridge: CUP. PDF also available online (Link retrieved on June 3, 2020): https://www.semanticscholar.org/paper/Keep-talking%3A-communicative-fluency-activities-for-Klippel/a5d8c237ba081195a1274a93cb11bce7ce894b02.

Krashen, S. (1981). *Second Language Acquisition and Second Language Learning*. Oxford: Pergamon.

Krashen, S. (1982). *Principles and Practice in Second Language Acquisition*. Pergamon: Oxford.

Krashen, S. (1985). *The Input Hypothesis: Issues and Implications*. New York: Longman.

Kwadzo, G. (2016). Développer la communication orale en français L2 en milieu autochtone: projet réalisé auprès d'apprenants de sixième année du primaire. In Allain, A. and P. Demers (Eds.). *Recherche et enseignement en milieu autochtone, La Revue de l'AQEFLS*, 32(1): pp. 76–87.

Lado, R. (1964). *Language Teaching: a Scientific Approach*. Ann Arbor: University of Michigan Press.

Lambert, W. and G. Tucker. (1972). *The Bilingual Education of Children: The St. Lambert Experiment*. Rowley: Newbury House.

Lanier, S. (2000). *Foreign to Familiar: a Guide to Understanding Hot-and-Cold Climate Cultures*. Hagerstown: McDougal.

Leblanc, R. (1990). *Étude nationale sur les programmes de français de base*. Ottawa: ACPLS.

Lemaire, E. (2021). Jeux de rôle et réconciliation avec les peuples autochtones. *Revue internationale de pédagogie de l'enseignement supérieur (Open Edition Journal En ligne)*, 37(1). Link retrieved on March 3, 2021: https://doi.org/10.4000/ripes.2988.

Lerède, J. (1983). *Suggérer pour apprendre*. Québec: Les Presses de l'Université du Québec.

Lozanov, G. (1978). *Suggestology and Outlines of Suggestopedia*. New York: Gordon Breach.

Madsen. H. (1983). *Techniques in Testing*. Oxford: Oxford University Press.

Maina, F. (1997). Culturally Relevant Pedagogy: First Nations Education in Canada. *The Canadian Journal of Natives Studies*, 17(2): pp. 293–314.

Mannavarayan, J.-M. (2002). *The French Immersion Debate*. Calgary: Detselig Enterprises Ltd.

Martindale, N. (2002). *The Cycle of Oppression and Distance Education.* Athabasca: Athabasca University.

Maxwell, W. (2014). *The Accelerative Integrated Methodology.* Online Article (Link retrieved on June 18, 2019): https://www.dropbox.com/s/x4cdembhaqzknzl/Wendy%27s%20article%20on%20the%20AIM%202%202014.docx?dl=0.

Mezirow, J. (1991). *Transformative Dimensions of Adult Learning.* San Francisco: Josey-Bass.

Netten, J. and C. Germain. (2012). Un nouveau paradigme pour l'apprentissage d'une langue seconde ou étrangère: l'approche neurolinguistique. *Neuroéducation,* 1(1): pp. 1–27.

Ontario Ministry of Education. (2021). *Indigenous Education Strategy.* Online Document (Link retrieved on March 7, 2021): gov.on.ca.

Osborne, A. (1996). Practice into Theory into Practice: Culturally Relevant Pedagogy for Students We Have Marginalised and Normalised. *Anthropology and Education Quarterly,* 27(3): pp. 285–314. Available online (Link retrieved on July 5, 2019): https://anthrosource.onlinelibrary.wiley.com/doi/abs/10.1525/aeq.1996.27.3.04x0351m.

Paradis, M. (2009). *Declarative and Procedural Determinants of Second Languages.* Amsterdam: John Benjamin.

Piaget, J. (1967). *La Psychologie de l'intelligence.* Paris: Armand Colin.

Proulx, A. (1996). *Une commission scolaire dans la cité.* Trois-Rivières: Commission scolaire de Trois-Rivières.

Pujyasri, C. (1991). *The Guru Tradition.* Mumbai: Bharatiya Vidya Bhavan.

Puren, C. (1988). *Histoire des méthodologies de l'enseignement des langues.* Paris: Clé international.

Puren, C. (2006). De l'approche communicative à la perspective actionnelle. *Le Français dans le monde,* 347: pp. 37–40.

Raham, H. (2009). *Best Practices in Aboriginal Education: A Literature Review and Analysis for Policy Directions.* On behalf of the Office of the Federal Interlocutor, Indian and Northern Affairs Canada. Report available online: (Link retrieved on July 9, 2019): http://www.firstpeoplesgroup.com/mnsiurban/PDF/education/Best_Practices_in_Aboriginal_Education-2009.pdf.

Rebuffot, J. (1993). *Le Point sur ... L'immersion au Canada.* Montréal: Centre éducatif et culturel Inc.

Rogers, C. (1969). *Freedom to Learn.* C. E. Merril: Columbus.

Rouss-Malpat, A. (2019). *Effectiveness of Explicit vs. Implicit L2 Instruction.* Doctoral dissertation. Published online (Link retrieved on June 11, 2019): https://www.dropbox.com/s/ealqjzkbmz4vrbx/AIM%20Dutch%20Research%202019.pdf?dl=0.

Ruhlen, M. (2007). *L'origine des langues.* Paris: Folio Essais.

Saladin d'Anglure, B. (2006). *Naître et renaître Inuit.* Paris: Gallimard.

Sapir, E. (1970). *Le langage.* Paris: Payot.

Saulis, M. (2019). *Indigegogy: Indigenous Education Model.* In Power Point Presentation given for the Canadian School Boards Association (CSBA) 2019 National Trustees Gathering on Indigenous Education: July 4, 2019.

de Saussure, F. (1965). *Cours de linguistique générale.* Paris: Payot.

Schumann. J. et al. (1978). Improvement of Foreign Language Pronunciation Under Hypnosis: A Preliminary Study. *Language Learning,* 28: pp. 143–148.

Skinner, F. (1957). *Verbal Behavior.* New York: Appleton-Century-Crafts.

Stern, H. (1984). *Fundamental Concepts of Language Teaching.* Oxford: Oxford University Press.

Tart, C. (1990). *Altered States of Consciousness.* San Francisco: Collins.

Toulouse, P. (n.d.). Supporting Aboriginal Student Success: Self-Esteem and Identity, A Living Teachings Approach. Online document. Link retrieved on May 3, 2021; dRead - Supporting Aboriginal Student Success: Self-Esteem and Identity, A Living Teachings Approach: Toulouse, Pamela Rose - desLibrisg .

Toulouse, P. (2011). *Achieving Aboriginal Student Success.* Winnipeg: Portage and Main. Also available online (Link retrieved on June 24, 2019): https://www.portageandmainpress.com/lesson_plans/plan_303_1.pdf.

Tremblay, R., M. Duplantie and D. Huot. (1999). *The Communicative-Experiential Syllabus.* Ottawa: ACPLS-CASLT. Available online (Link retrieved on June 17, 2019): https://www.caslt.org/files/pd/resources/research/1990-ncfs-2-communic-experien.pdf.

Tufts, A. (1998). *Pisukvigijait-Where You Walk: Inuit Students' Perceptions of Connections between Their Culture and School Science.* Unpublished M.Ed. thesis, University of New Brunswick.

Varga, C. (2014). *New Trends in Language Didactics-Noi direcții în didactica limbilor.* Cluj-Napoca: Presa Universitaria Clujeana.

Vygotsky L. (1978). *Mind in Society.* Harvard: Harvard University Press.

Walsh, R. (2011). *The World of Shamanism*. Woodbury: Llewellyn.

Watzlawick, P. (1984). *La réalité de la réalité*. Paris: Seuil.

Watzlawick, P., J. Beavin and D. Jackson. (1972). *Une Logique de la communication*. Paris: Seuil.

Winkin, Y. (2014). *La nouvelle communication*. Paris: Point.

Yang, J. (2012). The Affective Filter Hypothesis and Its Enlightenment for College English Teaching. *Psychology Research*, 07(2012) 1838—658X: pp. 40–43. Available online (Link retrieved on October 27, 2019): https://pdfs.semanticscholar.org/79dd/ffbe0c7b952369cee76803858b16dbe7bc05.pdf.

Yunkaporta, T. (2009). *Aboriginal Pedagogy at the Cultural Interface*. Doctoral dissertation. Available online (Link retrieved on August 16, 2019): https://researchonline.jcu.edu.au/10974/2/01thesis.pdf.

Annex I:

L2 Teaching to Aboriginal Learners in Québec

Historical Perspective

The history of L2 teaching in Québec can be divided in 4 periods.

1. The first period, the traditional Aboriginal teaching, had been used for times immemorial before the first contacts with European languages and cultures. Some European languages and cultures were and are still dominant languages and cultures. Those dominant languages and cultures for the Americas are Dutch, English, French, Portuguese and Spanish.
2. As already mentioned, the first dominant language taught to Aboriginal learners in Canada was French. As a matter of fact, the first French L2 courses were given in Trois-Rivières in 1616. In those days, the method used to teach a L2 belonged to the classical paradigm and the emphasis was put on writing, grammar and vocabulary. The main purposes of that teaching were to civilize and Christianize Aboriginal peoples.
3. In 1879, the Canadian Parliament decided that Catholic and Protestant religious residential schools would be responsible to teach L2 dominant languages to young Aboriginal learners. That period covers more than one century as the closing year of the last residential school was 1996[50] in Punnichy, near Regina, in Saskatchewan.
4. In the last part of the twentieth century, Aboriginal communities in Québec started to take the education system in their own hands. Every nation has its own way of doing it. For example, the Inuit and

---

[50] Most authors mention 1996 as the last year of the Aboriginal residential school system.

the Cree have their own school boards, the Kativik School Board for the Inuit and the Cree School Board for the Cree. Aboriginals also have their own college, the Kiuna College. All those institutions offer courses in Aboriginal languages and the two dominant languages of Québec, English and French.

Geographical Perspective

There are two groups of Aboriginal People in Québec, the Inuit and the First Nations, since the Québec government does not recognize the Métis Nation of Québec.

The Aboriginal communities of Québec are the Abenaki, the Anishinaabeg, the Attikamekw, the Cree, the Maliseet, the Mi'kmaq, the Innu, the Inuit, the Mohawk, the Naskapi and the Wendat.

The importance of the dominant language, French or English and sometimes both depends on geographic ties each nation had with either French or English settlers, missionaries and traders. For example the word for '*cat*' in Northern Cree is '*bushush*' from the English '*pussy*' (in '*pussycat*') while in Southern Cree, the word for '*cat*' is '*minoush*' from the French word '*minou*', a familiar word for '*cat*', because in the past, Northern Cree had more contacts with the English traders and missionaries than the Southern Cree who had more contacts with the French traders and missionaries.

That is why, different dominant languages are taught and used by Aboriginal communities in Québec.

French is taught and used by the following Aboriginal nations of Québec: the Abenaki, the Attikamekh, the Innu, the Maliseet[51] and the Wendat. English is taught and used by the following Aboriginal nations of Québec: the Cree, the Mi'kmaq, the Mohawk, the Inuit and the Naskapi.

French and English are taught and used by the Anishinaabeg, depending on the communities.

Every nation also has an Aboriginal language. Knowledge and use of their traditional language vary a great deal among the nations and the communities. For example, almost every Inuit speaks his or her

---

[51] Another Maliseet nation uses French outside of Québec: the Madawaska Maliseet Nation, near Edmundston, New Brunswick.

traditional language, while very few Abenaki speak their traditional language. That situation can be explained by the proximity of towns: if an Aboriginal community is close to a town, chances are that the dominant language (French or English) will be used by members of that Aboriginal community.

However, revitalization of their traditional language and culture is a very important aspect of every Aboriginal education system in Québec at least since the last part of the twentieth century. Aboriginal writers, singers and filmmakers use more and more their own language.

Annex II:

Teaching French L2 to Different L1 Learners

Teaching French L2 to Anglophones or English speakers, Allophones or immigrants of different L1 and Aboriginal learners differs.

English speakers have a strong linguistic and cultural identity. Their mother tongue being widely spoken all over the world and their culture being dominant in many countries of the world, their identity is not threatened by French language and culture. Like speakers of other strong L1s such as Mandarin and Spanish, they have no fear of loosing their L1 or their C1 (native culture). They may be afraid of making mistakes, but making them will not affect their identity. However, because of that, they might have the tendency not to correct their mistakes as much as someone who has a less dominant language would. That is why they may develop an interlanguage of their own that is often very difficult to correct, as already mentioned in the book. Developing an interlanguage is, in fact, a natural phenomenon because learners try to learn a new language by using what they already know, their mother tongue. However, with the communicative methods, they may not try to correct their speech as long as they can communicate. The interlanguage of English speakers learning French is full of English structures, expressions and vocabulary. Nevertheless if English speakers learn French with learners of different mother tongues, their interlanguage will differ from the one of English speakers learning French in a group of English speakers.

The same thing is true for Spanish speakers learning French in a group of Spanish learners. This is the reason why immigrant learners learning French L2 and who have different mother tongues, as if it often the case, will not develop a strong interlanguage as their different L1s will impact on French in different ways. Their only way to communicate will be to use French and if they use expressions coming from their L1, communication will not be accurate and the communication process may be interrupted.

They will use French to negotiate meaning. This phenomenon is true for language structures, words, expressions and pronunciation.

Aboriginal learners learning French L2 may feel threatened by the language and the culture learned. Indeed, they may feel threatened when learning a dominant language no matter what the language is.

Annex III:

IPA Transcriptions of the Québec Cree

The transcription of the Québec Cree phonemes in IPA symbols by the author was not an easy task to do.

Indeed, if it is possible to find on the Internet IPA symbols for diverse varieties of Cree, including Plains Cree, it was not possible to find IPA symbols for the Québec Crees. As the phonological system differs from one variety of Cree to another (that is the main reason why a variety differs from another variety), the author first had to listen carefully to the sounds of the Québec Cree, represented by the Cree syllabics that was on the Internet site of the Cree School Board. Then, the author had to consult two native speakers of Cree (one speaker of the Northern variety and one speaker of the Southern variety) to clarify certain sounds that were not clear enough to be transcribed in the IPA symbols. The native speakers were Mrs. Lucy Shem from the Cree community of Chisasibi for the Northern variety and Mrs. Rose Dixon Gilpin from the Cree community of Waswanipi for the Southern variety, Those two native speakers were then education consultants for the Cree School Board and the author wishes to thank them for their cooperation.

It must be underlined here that other Algonkien languages of Québec, such as Innu and Naskapi that some linguists consider as Cree language varieties were not taken into account. Only the Crees spoken in the communities of the Cree School Board were considered. The Northern variety of the Québec Cree is spoken is the following Cree communities: Whapgoostui, Chisasibi, Wemingi and Eastmain. The Southern variety of the Québec Cree is spoken in the communities of Waskaganish, Nemaska, Mistissini, Ouje-Bougoumou, Waswanipi. However, the differences between those varieties of Cree are minimal and a speaker of one variety can easily understand a speaker from the other variety while a speaker of a more geographically distant variety such as Plains Cree will be less understandable by a Québec Cree speaker.

Québec Cree Phonemes

Northern Variety (20 phonemes)
Consonants (14 phonemes)
m n p t tʃ ʃ k θ s ɹ j w l h
Vowels (6 phonemes)
I ɪ ɔ u a ɑ
Southern Variety (17 phonemes)
Consonants (12 phonemes)
m n p t k θ s ɹ j w l h
Vowels (5 phonemes)
I ɪ ɔ u ɛ

Afterword

When I started teaching English L2 at the Cree School Board in 2003, I already had a long L2 teaching experience to English speakers and immigrants.

As a member of the *Québec* Métis Nation, I was especially exited when I realized that at this First Nation's institution, we were dealing with three languages: Cree, English and French. As I had been interested in linguistics all my professional life, I felt this new job would be a challenging one and indeed it was!

First, I discovered that although we were dealing with three languages, the languages were not perceived as equal. Over French, English was seen as more important. Even over Cree, English was seen as more important. In fact, it seemed that English was the only important language and some people wanted to abolish the teaching of Cree while other people wanted to abolish the teaching of French. However, nobody suggested that the teaching of English should be abolished. English was the most important language. It still is.

Almost twenty years later, teachers of the Cree School Board still teach English, Cree and French, but English is still the dominant language, even though Cree is now more taught than it was twenty years ago. I am not surprised by that, but I find it sad.

I could always relate to my Cree colleagues and students because as a proud Métis Quebecer and a native speaker of French, I also felt threatened by English, the dominant language of Canada.

In fact, as a native French language speaker, I still feel threatened by the dominance of English in Canada and, of course, speakers of Aboriginal languages in Canada should also feel threatened by English.

Indeed, in a white paper presented in 2021, the federal government of Canada itself recognizes the fact that French is threatened by English in Canada. Indeed, Her Majesty the Queen in Right of Canada (2021, p. 6) says:

The development of digital technology and international trade is favoring the use of English. As a result, the use of French is declining in Canada and its vitality is a cause for concern.

So, the fundamental reason why I felt I wanted to write this book is probably because I am convinced that all languages and cultures should be given a chance to survive and evolve and that they should be shown respect. Therefore, teaching a dominant language should always be done in a respectful way for the learner's threatened language and culture.

Book Summary

For an Aboriginal, to learn a foreign or second dominant language such as English, French or Spanish, can constitute a threat to his or her identity.

The book presents a theoretical framework for different second and foreign language didactics paradigms used today in second or foreign language teaching and describes practical procedures and techniques that can be used with Aboriginal learners with respect to their own language, identity, cultural values and traditions.

The emphasis is put on the radical paradigm because it is this paradigm that best answers Aboriginal learners needs.

About the Author

A *Québec* Métis, Pierre Demers holds a Ph.D. in Education from the *Université de Montréal*.

For many years, he has been working in French and English as an administrator, consultant, professor, researcher, teacher and facilitator. He worked in several Canadian provinces and overseas, from elementary to university levels. Among other things, he taught English, French and Literacy to Bush People, adults born and raised in the *Québec* taiga. He delivered and published several papers and gave numerous workshops on language teaching to Aboriginal learners.

He retired from the *Université du Québec* and the Cree School Board, a First Nation institution in Northern *Québec*.

He is now a part-time lecturer in Education at the *Université Sainte Anne*, an Acadian institution in Nova Scotia, and a freelance consultant for language teaching to Aboriginal learners.

Champs didactiques plurilingues : données pour des politiques stratégiques

La recherche scientifique en sciences sociales et humaines contribue à fournir des données utiles à la prise de décision dans les organisations (administrations publiques et établissements, entreprises ou associations, à des niveaux locaux, régionaux, nationaux, internationaux). Dans le domaine de l'appropriation des langues étrangères, cette constitution d'informations étayées est d'autant plus nécessaire que les enjeux liés aux flux de population et de communication, à l'insertion des populations dans le développement par l'éducation, la formation et l'emploi et à l'aménagement des relations entre les langues par des politiques linguistiques éducatives et universitaires stratégiques deviennent chaque jour plus urgents.

Pour répondre à ce besoin, la collection vise à promouvoir les travaux et recherches autour de l'enseignement / apprentissage des langues étrangères, dans une perspective de mise en évidence du triple ancrage social sujets – objets – contextes ainsi que de leurs dynamiques propres et interagissantes. Il s'agit de prendre en compte comme domaines de connaissance l'ensemble des champs disciplinaires impliqués dans la production de savoirs pratiques et théoriques et comme terrains, l'ensemble des situations concrètes, des situations d'apprentissage et des situations professionnelles d'enseignement ainsi que les politiques linguistiques éducatives et universitaires, qui influent sur les activités d'appropriation de telle ou telle langue, sur leur choix et sur leur statut.

Elle s'adresse à la communauté de chercheurs en didactique des langues et à leurs étudiants, aux acteurs éducatifs et aux décideurs institutionnels qui y trouveront des données et des analyses pour alimenter leurs capacités décisionnelles et organisationnelles.

La collection se déploie sur deux volets : un volet « La recherche en mouvement » destiné aux chercheurs, aux étudiants-chercheurs et aux praticiens-chercheurs, comme le sont un certain nombre d'enseignants par exemple ; un volet « Savoirs pour savoir faire » destiné plus particulièrement aux étudiants, aux praticiens et aux décideurs.

Directeur de collection : Patrick Chardenet

Comité scientifique

Maria Helena Araújo e Sá, Universidade de Aveiro (Portugal)
Philippe Blanchet, Université de Haute Bretagne Rennes 2 (France)
Jean-Marc Defays, Université de Liège (Belgique)
Christain Degache, Universidade Federal do Minais Gerais / Université Grenoble Alpes (Brésil / France)
Fred Dervin, Helsingfors Uniersitet (Finlande)
Piet Desmet, Katholieke Universite it Leuven (Belgique)
Olivier Dezutter, Université de Sherbrooke (Canada)
Enrica Galazzi, Università Cattolica del Sacro Cuore (Italie)
Laurent Gajo, Université de Genève (Suisse)
Tony Liddicoat, University of Warwick (Royaume Uni)
Eliane Lousada, Universidade de São Paulo (Brésil)
Bruno Maurer, Université Paul Valéry, Montpellier 3 (France)
Dominique Macaire, Université de Lorraine (France)
Danièle Moore, Simon Fraser University (Canada)
Christian Ollivier, Université de La Réunion (France)
Fabián Santiago, Université Paris 8 Vincennes - Saint-Denis & CNRS (France)
Haydée Silva, Universidad Nacional Autónoma de México (Mexique)

Ouvrage parus

Savoirs pour savoir faire

Vol. 1 – Laurent Puren et Bruno Maurer (dir.), *La crise de l'apprentissage en Afrique francophone subsaharienne. Regards croisés sur la didactique des langues et les pratiques enseignantes.* 2018.

Vol. 3 – Kaouthar Ben Abdallah et Mohamed Embarki, *Éducation et formation en contexte plurilingue maghrébin. Problématiques entre didactique et politique linguistique éducative.* 2020.

Vol. 4 – Maria Helena Araújo e Sá & Carla Maria Ataíde Maciel (eds.), *Interculturalidade e plurilinguismo nos discursos e práticas de educação e formação. Contextos pós-coloniais de língua portuguesa.* 2021.

La recherche en mouvement

Vol. 2 – Jue Wang Szilas, *Apprendre des langues distantes en eTandem. Une étude de cas dans un dispositif universitaire sino-francophone.* 2020.

Vol. 5 – Pierre Demers, *Elements of Second and Foreign Languages Teaching to Indigenous Learners of Canada. Theories, Strategies and Practices.* 2021.

www.peterlang.com

www.ingramcontent.com/pod-product-compliance
Lightning Source LLC
Chambersburg PA
CBHW061718300426
44115CB00014B/2739